All About
The Bus Ministry

By Dr. Wally Beebe
Sword of the Lord Publishers
Box 1099
Murfreesboro, Tennessee 37130

Copyright, 1970
Sword of the Lord Publishers

This printing: 1974
Accumulated total 101,000
Price: $1.25

Printed in U.S.A.

DEDICATION

This book is dedicated to the great men who worked with me as bus captains:

Mr. Hank Andrews
Mr. Raymond Appleby
Mr. Stuart Blong
Mr. Fred Bullington
Mr. Norman Burleson
Mr. Billy Eatmon
Mr. O. M. Gunnells
Mr. Les Gilmore
Mr. Glenn LaVanchy
Mr. Jesse Maynor
Mr. John Mints
Mr. Charles Oswalt
Mr. Don Sass
Mr. Larry Schweckendieck
Mr. Derril Smith
Mr. David Williams

PREFACE

Have you ever wondered what you could do—

1. About children who are willing to come to church and parents who aren't?
2. About whom to get for new teachers and soul winners in your church?
3. About the fact you have prepared a salvation message and see no one unsaved present?
4. About the deadness of reaction during your invitation?
5. About the preacher boy in your church who wants to serve the Lord?
6. About the decline in your membership by moving away and death?

The answer to the above question is *the bus ministry.* The following book is designed to help the preacher and Christian worker to see the possibilities of reaching beyond his immediate neighborhood in his scope of soul-winning vision.

During the past few years it has been my pleasure to start or revitalize bus ministries in such churches as Trinity Baptist Church, Jacksonville, Florida (running about 1,000 to 1,100 on buses); Thomas Road Baptist Church, Lynchburg, Virginia; Gospel Light Baptist Church, Walkertown, North Carolina; Northside Baptist Church, Charlotte, North Carolina; Woodland Baptist Church, Winston-Salem, North Carolina; and many others. All of these churches average in Sunday school well above the 1,000 mark. Some are country churches and others are city churches. I have set up this simple system in churches having anywhere from 40 to 3,000 in Sunday school. It will work in rural, city, large, or small churches. In the rural church of which I am now pastor, this system, after three months of application, brought the bus ministry from 30 to 360. Another new church went from 40 to 196 in Sunday school in 7 weeks using this system.

It is my prayer that this book may be helpful to every pastor and Christian worker who wants to embark on the bus ministry or to improve the ministry he already has.

TABLE OF CONTENTS

Chapter   Page

1. Background. 11
2. Motivation 14
   The Why of the Bus Ministry 14
   Why Not?. 14
   The Why. 17
3. Preparation. 23
   1. Check on Prospect Areas 23
      Quantity. 25
      Do Bus Routes Pay?. 26
      Distance of Routes 26
   2. Secure a Bus 28
      What Size? 32
      What Shape?. 33
      Where?. 35
   3. The Key, the Bus Captains 37
      Captains or Pastors? 38
      Getting the Key. 39
      Strange Creatures 41
   4. Additional Help 42
   5. Policy. 43
4. Implementation. 46
   1. Visit the Bus Route. 47
      Easy Canvass 48
      Several Basic Ways. 48
      Soul Winning Later. 51
      Smile. 54

    Sample Visit for Regulars 55
    Sample Call for New Ones 59
    Electrical Cut-In Call 59
    Goals. 62
 2. Contests 63
    Contests for Kids. 64
    Contests for Captains 67
 3. Keeping Records. 68
    Bus Captains' Records 71
Last Words 76
Examples of People Saved 79
5. Individual Questions and Comments. 83

INTRODUCTION

To First Edition

Wally Beebe is a ten-talented man. Not the least of these talents is his ability to organize a great bus ministry and enlist people to spend themselves in the carrying out of his plans.

May God give this book a wide circulation and may those who read and hear be doers of the Word.

The bus ministry that he leads at the great Trinity Baptist Church of Jacksonville, Florida, under the direction of its Pastor, Dr. Bob Gray, is a challenging and inspiring one. Every pastor and Christian worker would do well to consider the thoughts and ideas contained herein.

April, 1968   DR. JACK HYLES, Pastor
                                 First Baptist Church
                                 Hammond, Indiana

Chapter 1

Background

Several years ago while I was pastor of Grace Baptist Church, Kankakee, Illinois, I saw a short paragraph in a book about a bus ministry. Then I saw a denominational periodical that mentioned a bus ministry in a church with a picture of the buses. That formulated an idea for the same thing in my city. I thought to myself, "Wouldn't it be wonderful to bring in an extra hundred people each Sunday on buses?"

I purchased one bus, then another, then a third. Although we had the largest bus ministry in our city, I felt that it was not a tremendous success. I had zeal without knowledge. On the best day which we ever had we only averaged about twenty per bus. The buses were not being run in a systematic plan with a motive and an objective. A pastor of one of the churches where I conducted a bus seminar confessed to me that for years he had been trying to figure out how to get rid of the one bus that he owned. Now he has a great bus ministry bringing in hundreds to his services each week and souls are being saved constantly. Just having the vehicles in the church yard is not enough. One must know exactly how to use them or they are no good to you.

After some three and a half years in this pastorate I joined Dr. Bob Gray as his associate at the famous Trinity Baptist Church in Jacksonville, Florida. On approximately the first anniversary of my being with

Dr. Gray he placed me in charge of the bus ministry. We had at that time five buses carrying between 150 and 170 persons per Sunday.

When I was placed in charge, I wrote to those who had leading bus ministries—Dr. Jack Hyles of the First Baptist Church of Hammond, Indiana (at that time running 600 or so on 17 buses); and to Dr. J. R. Faulkner, co-pastor of the Highland Park Baptist Church of Chattanooga, Tennessee (at that time running 11 buses consistently—although the Sunday I wrote him he had 900 on 17 buses). Dr. Lee Roberson is the pastor of this latter great church.

After digesting the replies I checked for books on the subject of buses and found none. There were several on soul-winning topics that alluded to buses but none on how to do it.

I discovered from these men and others some basic principles, ideas, and methods that revolutionized our bus ministry at Trinity and brought bus attendance up from 170 on my first Sunday to an average of 750 at the writing of this book. (At the second edition of this book the bus ministry at Trinity is running an average of 1,000 to 1,100 per Sunday; and they have had as many as 1,360 on 22 buses on one particular Sunday.) Yes, these things work! They will not only revolutionize your bus work but your entire church will be stirred and blessed! We have more people saved through this ministry than through all of the missionaries we support on the foreign field combined. It is the best financial investment per dollar for souls that a person can make.

The attendance in buses as far as who is first or second in the nation will sometimes be between two or three churches. Therefore, I will not attempt to list the churches in the order of their bus attendance because I would have to have a report from the past Sunday to find out which one was in reality in first, or second, or third, etc., place. Approximately, the first five churches in America that we know of that are definitely using buses are the First Baptist Church, Hammond, Indiana; Landmark Baptist Temple, Cincinnati, Ohio; Trinity Baptist Church, Jacksonville, Florida; Canton Baptist Temple, Canton, Ohio; Highland Park Baptist Church, Chattanooga, Tennessee.

Because of their size there are a number of churches that use their buses in the same way a company uses a salesman on commission. They are not necessarily striving for a great average per bus. Instead they go at it with the idea that they will give anyone a bus and if he brings in 10, or 15, or 20 people who were not there last week, that will, of course, help the overall attendance of the church; and provide unsaved souls who will be responsive to the Gospel. In a real sense every bus captain is a salesman for that church.

At Trinity we strove to have a high attendance average per bus because we had a limited budget for buses. Therefore, I believe that we had, and they maintain today, the largest average per bus of any church in America. We were constantly trying to refine the ministry of the buses and help it to operate more smoothly and attain better averages per Sunday. The small church starting out would do well to follow this example to get a great number on a few buses to conserve finances. In our present pastorate a few weeks ago we had 469 on 6 buses; an average of 78 per bus (after 10 months of applying this method).

Another feature of the bus ministry that is a blessing, besides the others that have been mentioned and will be mentioned, is that many churches have parking problems, and, although they would like to grow, they do not have the parking space to bring in automobiles for every two or three people who attend. Consequently, it is extremely practical to have bus ministries that bring in 50 or 60 people on one bus and take a great deal less space as far as parking is concerned.

Chapter 2

Motivation

I wish to suggest at the beginning of this book that as you read it you underline certain portions that give facts that pertain to the questions you have about your particular bus setup or route. I would also suggest that you go back and read this through at least two or more times after the first reading and try to get the _psychology of the bus ministry_. Then stick to the various things that have been mentioned here in the book. A pastor, who asked my advice regarding revitalizing his bus ministry, reported after using these suggestions for six weeks his bus ministry was increased by approximately 165 people. The following is a quote from his letter: "The bus captains are using almost to the letter your advice and we find it works and there is a lot of enthusiasm among them." That Sunday they averaged 65 per bus on their buses.

THE WHY OF THE BUS MINISTRY

In any project both the negative and positive must be considered. First, let us consider *why not* to have a bus ministry.

WHY NOT?

There are several wrong reasons _and_ unworthy

motivations for the bus ministry being started in your church. Here are some.

1. It is wrong to start a bus ministry as a status symbol or because everyone else is doing it. To be able to go to the preachers' meeting and say that you have a bus ministry does not mean that the Lord has led you into such an endeavor, any more than the Lord leads everyone to start schools, rescue missions, deaf works, television ministries, radio ministries, etc.

2. It is wrong to start a bus ministry just to boost your attendance and not with the bus passengers' individual welfare in mind. For instance, some churches say, "We need to push for two or three hundred more in our attendance so that everyone will think we are growing." However, neither the church, the people, nor the pastor consider the bus people as part of their church; nor are they concerned about anything except boosting the attendance number. This sometimes results in churches biting off more than they can chew in that when they get the bus people into the church they do not know where to put them because they are ashamed of them. The numbers in attendance must be realized as being souls. Each number represents one soul for whom Christ died. This must be kept uppermost in our minds.

3. It is wrong to start a bus ministry simply to compete with another church out of ecclesiastical jealousy.

4. It is wrong to start a bus ministry simply to find a way to spend some money that you have accumulated in a home mission's account. It is also wrong to use the bus ministry and the dear people involved in it as a fund-raising appeal. Some have started orphanages because they realize that everyone loves an orphan or have started homes for alcoholics because they know that everyone feels sorry for a drunkard and his family. Unless we are concerned about the souls involved we ought to leave them alone. There are a number of drawbacks in a bus ministry. Any pastor who launches such a

ministry must take care of all the people he brings into the church through this ministry. For example, when a church assumes the responsibility for these children it must realize there will be family problems, fights, conflicts, drinking problems, fathers that won't provide for the family, mothers who will leave home, and many other things of a similar nature in the home life of the people involved that will have to be ironed out by the Sunday school teachers, bus captains, and the pastor.

I recall one of our bus people who used to call me every time he was arrested and put in jail for drinking. When you multiply that by the number of routes you have and people on the routes that would have that problem you will have a lot of phones ringing. I recall also the time one of our ladies called Dr. Gray and myself to take her to the hospital to have her tenth child while her husband was out of town driving a truck.

I have run into some people we would call "deadbeats" on some bus routes. These are folks who constantly require groceries and handouts because the father does not work and stays drunk most of the time. This may involve fuel oil, clothing, and furniture for the families. I do not advise any bus ministry, started or just starting, to be in the business of social rehabilitation and the placement of used furniture and God's money on a bus route. (We have had to, of necessity, acquire quantities of used clothing to fit men, women, boys, and girls to give to the bus route people. It might be wise to designate a room in your church where ladies could size, iron, and sort these clothes and have them ready so a bus captain and his wife could bring the people to the church to outfit them with enough clothes so that they could at least attend the services.)

Anyone launching a program of a bus ministry must be willing to take the people exactly as they are and try to get them saved and to win the family and parents for Christ. One of our bus captains the other day started

16

to pick up four little children in front of a house. They all came out wearing brand new shorts and no shoes. The bus captain kindly said, "That's all right. You can put your shoes on in the bus." The children looked mystified and answered him with a strange expression on their faces as they said, "Mister, we don't have any shoes." Naturally, these children were welcome as they came.

Anyone starting a bus route must realize that this will probably bring barefoot children into the church and will account for a lot more rowdiness in the service plus people who may not smell too good nor look too good. It will definitely amount to a great deal more time and effort put in by the pastor of such a church as he ministers to the increased number of people and families brought in by the buses. We have now mentioned several reasons why you should *not* have a bus ministry and some of the drawbacks involved in one; but let us mention the positive side also.

THE WHY

The why of a bus ministry is as old as the Great Commission itself in that we are to go into the highways and hedges and compel them to come in to hear the Gospel and be saved!

1. The first *why* is to reach lost people who are not saved! Any pastor starting a bus ministry could preach for many weeks on soul winning before the ministry starts in order to get his people challenged along the line of winning souls with this particular ministry. Here are just a few passages of Scripture that teach us that the bus ministry is as scriptural as the Gospel.

"But when he saw the multitudes, he was moved with compassion on them, because they fainted, and were scattered abroad, as sheep having no shepherd. Then

saith he unto his disciples, The harvest truly is plenteous, but the labourers are few; Pray ye therefore the Lord of the harvest, that he will send forth labourers into his harvest." — Matt. 9:36-38.

Here, the Lord Jesus tells us there are multitudes of people that need to be saved and, yes, want to be saved. But, the problem is not with the multitude of unsaved people; it is with the sorry Christian who will not go and tell them how to be saved or bring them physically to the church so they may hear the Gospel preached in the power of the Holy Spirit. The "Beebe" translation of the last two verses would read like this: 'Then saith he unto his disciples, The harvest truly is plenteous, but the bus captains are few; Pray ye therefore the Lord of the harvest that he will send forth bus captains into all the lanes of the country and the city to bring in the harvest.'

"The blind receive their sight, and the lame walk, the lepers are cleansed, and the deaf hear, the dead are raised up, AND THE POOR HAVE THE GOSPEL PREACHED TO THEM." — Matt. 11:5.

The discouraged John the Baptist sits in prison and sends an inquiry to Jesus to ask if He is the Christ. Jesus replies that they are to go and show John again the things that they had heard and seen. The list follows in verse 5 that I have just quoted for you. Next to the raising of the dead, Jesus said the miracle that will prove that I am really the Christ is the fact that the Gospel is preached to the poor. What a tremendous commentary this is on modern-day churches who laugh at the poor and shun to have them in the services! Jesus said this was one of the miracles that proved He was the Christ. Jesus and those who would follow Him would preach the Gospel to poor people.

Within the first few years of Dr. Jack Hyles' great ministry at First Baptist Church in Hammond, Indiana,

Dr. Hyles had to take a stand on a number of issues and there was an ensuing separation of some of the members of the church. As Dr. Hyles gave the program on which he would build the great soul-winning work that has come out of this church, one of his points was, "The rich and the poor shall be welcomed equally at our church." Many of the folks that we will reach on the bus routes will be poor people and those who would otherwise never hear the Gospel because of the unconcern of most churches.

Matthew 13, verse 38 says, "The field is the world ...." When you embark on a bus ministry there will no doubt be phone calls that you will receive from neighboring pastors talking to you about staying in your own "field." Jesus said, "*The field is the world.*" Someday if we wish to win souls we may have to run buses to the moon or to some other distant place. We are allowed by the Lord Jesus to invade every area of the landscape in order to find souls who need to be saved and bring them to Christ. This is a perfectly legitimate and scriptural endeavor.

"*And whoso shall receive one such little child in my name receiveth me.... Take heed that ye despise not one of these little ones; for I say unto you, That in heaven their angels do always behold the face of my Father which is in heaven. For the Son of man is come to save that which was lost.*"—Matt. 18:5,10,11.

Christ laid great stress on children and wanted them to also hear His teaching and be received by Christians.

"*Then were there brought unto him little children, that he should put his hands on them, and pray: and the disciples rebuked them. But Jesus said, Suffer little children, and forbid them not, to come unto me: for of such is the kingdom of heaven.*"—Matt. 19:13,14.

"*Go ye therefore into the highways, and as many as*

ye shall find, bid to the marriage. So those servants went out into the highways, and gathered together all as many as they found, both bad and good: and the wedding was furnished with guests." — Matt. 22:9,10.

"So that servant came, and shewed his lord these things. Then the master of the house being angry said to his servant, Go out quickly into the streets and lanes of the city, and bring in hither the poor, and the maimed, and the halt, and the blind. And the servant said, Lord, it is done as thou hast commanded, and yet there is room. And the lord said unto the servant, Go out into the highways and hedges, and compel them to come in, that my house may be filled." — Luke 14:21-23.

The Lord Jesus seems to be telling us over and over again that we need to go out and get people to come to hear the Gospel and to come to the wedding feast of the Lamb. In the bus ministry you will be using contests that offer rewards. Some will criticize this but Jesus has said to compel them to come in. Matthew 10:42 additionally says,

"And whosoever shall give to drink unto one of these little ones a cup of cold water only in the name of a disciple, verily I say unto you, he shall in no wise lose his reward."

Our Lord could have said that it would be a nice thing for us to do this deed or that it was a noble thing for us to do this deed but instead He appealed to the *carnal* motives of man in that He said you will receive a reward for doing these deeds in My name. Therefore, if Christ can hold out rewards for cups of cold water surely we can give out bubble gum, penny candy, goldfish, and all other manner of paraphernalia in order to get a child to come and hear the Gospel of Christ and issue him a reward.

2. The second *why* is to *provide transportation* for

those who would not get to the service otherwise. When most people start a bus ministry they envision a great number of small vans darting out from the church in all directions to shuttle people back and forth from their homes and provide free transportation for those who are interested in coming. Nothing could be farther from the truth! <u>Basically the bus ministry is *not* a matter of transportation! It is a matter of PERSONAL INTEREST</u>. I will illustrate this now and emphasize it later. Please erase from your mind the idea that the bus ministry is simply transportation for people who have no other way to get to church. In many of the homes that you will contact they will have as many as two cars in the yard but would never drive one of them to any church service. I have many times visited homes across the street from churches and asked them if they attended church anywhere and found out they didn't. I have then lined them up to ride a bus for forty-five minutes or an hour to our church which was in another city or another section of the city. Is it then a matter of transportation? No! If it were, the person would walk across the street to go to the church that is closest but instead he chooses to go with the person who shows *personal interest* in either himself or his children. Therefore, please <u>forget the idea that it is actually transportation</u>. (In a few cases it will be a matter of transportation because you will find some widows who do not have a car or funds to come and there will be some homes where the car is out of town or with the husband at work. I have also seen a very few cases where the family car was broken down and the people came on the bus for this reason. Also, there are poor people who would not have private transportation nor the finances to ride the public transportation.)

3. <u>The third *why* is to make the local church as close as your street</u>. The old idea of a community church in a neighborhood is a thing of the past. People

drive to the other side of town to buy groceries and will ride a public conveyance for blocks in order to purchase some item at a sale price. Why then should people not be provided transportation to another part of the city in order to attend a Bible-believing church that will deliver something for the spiritual needs. In one sense of the word, each bus becomes a mobile chapel bringing the people into the main church for the services. The bus ride is simply the opening exercises for their Sunday school class. Also, in a sense of the word, the bus captain becomes a real arm of the church going into the particular community that he has been assigned to. (On some of our buses we have a song leader who will lead the children in choruses to keep them occupied as they ride to the church services.)

Chapter 3

Preparation

1. CHECK ON PROSPECT AREAS

Our first portion of preparation would be to find a prospective area in your city that would accommodate a bus route. I've mentioned the word city but do not mean to eliminate the country church from a bus route possibility. Rev. Raymond Hancock of the Providence Baptist Church at Riverview, Florida, has a very going bus ministry with some 10 buses bringing in 400 per Sunday to his Sunday school and church. This church is located in a crossroads way out in the country away from all cities. Rev. Bobby Roberson, Gospel Light Baptist Church, Rural Route, Walkertown, North Carolina, has a country church that is located in the middle of a cornfield and runs some 1200 average attendance with three to four hundred coming on the buses. A country church can have a successful bus ministry by going down all of the highways and side roads and sometimes going into the little cities or villages near the church. Basically, you should get a good map of your area and then drive through the sections of the area probably closest to your church first. I have seen some cases where the first bus routes were started in a radius of 10 to 15 miles away from the church in a fruitful area that would yield many children and then the areas between there and the church were worked thoroughly until the routes were right on the doorstep of the church.

(The following paragraph changed one bus captain from bringing in 12 to bringing in 143 in the period of six weeks on his bus. Read it carefully and get the concept.)

Homes in the twenty to thirty-thousand dollars category would be very difficult (but not impossible) to enlist for children on a bus ministry. The church that is just starting a bus ministry (unless your entire area is in a higher class or higher financial strata), should try to reach a slummy area of the city. I received word just recently of a large church that is having good success in new subdivisions and apartment buildings that are in the <u>higher financial bracket but for the most part this would be unadvisable for many churches</u> to try as their first bus venture. You are looking for houses where the windows are not all in and there is a cardboard over a broken pane, where the plastic curtains are waving in the breeze out the broken window, where the front glass of the door has been broken out and a piece of linoleum has been tacked in its place, where the screen door has been broken out by the children who have been playing, where the area around the door handle is black with finger marks made by little children who have been trying to get in the door, where there are broken toys, swing sets, play things that indicate children live in the home. You are looking for a place where there is a preeminence of junk in the yard, possibly an old car or two up on blocks, and lots of children. You are looking for a place where a lot of people live, possibly an apartment building, or trailer court, or housing project. <u>Any place where there is a great concentration of populace is the best place for a bus ministry</u>...particularly the <u>lower class and lower financial section</u> of town.

Quantity

You are always interested in *people* above all else on a bus ministry. The philosophy of a bus ministry may be summed up by the one word, *quantity*. After giving a bus lecture in the Thomas Road Baptist Church, Lynchburg, Virginia, one of the bus captains came up to me and told me a short story. He had been reading this book and had listened to the bus lecture where I emphasized this point, that we were looking for poor homes. He had purchased a van to start the bus ministry himself and had been bringing from 6 to 12 in on this van for several months. He had been visiting in the area in which his home was located which was a new subdivision of $20,000.00 and up homes. He was quite discouraged. This young man came enthusiastically to tell me that he felt he had been doing it wrong and wanted some advice. With a few more words we had discussed the place of the bus ministry as far as prospect area was concerned and he said, "This is exactly the kind of place where I work." He conveyed to me that he was a postman and worked in an area that was going down quite rapidly. There was a mixture of races in the area and many folks were moving out of the area. Large and stately looking homes had been chopped up into several apartments and had deteriorated a great deal. This tremendous bus captain was Preston Morris. Preston and I visited on the bus route and on the first Sunday after changing his area he had 35 on his route. The next Sunday 67, the next Sunday 93, the next Sunday 78, the next Sunday 126, the next Sunday 143. This means that in six weeks after seeing this one point this man went from approximately 12 on his van to 143! Preston Morris found that he had a God-given ability to start bus routes and the wise pastor, Dr. Jerry Falwell, "loosed him and let him go." Now Preston is engaged in starting new bus routes constantly and training workers so that they in turn can take over the routes after he gets them started.

Do Bus Routes Pay?

Right here let me say that the bus ministry is not a way to finance your church. If a person starts a bus route and thinks the people will pay for it themselves with the nickels and dimes the children bring on the bus, they are badly mistaken. This project must be taken on as a *home missions'* project because there is no great ratio of a bus ministry paying for itself in its initial stages. Dr. Bob Jones, Sr., said, "If you will emphasize the spiritual, God will take care of the financial." This has always been my experience in the starting of many hundreds of bus routes around America. God will encourage your people to give more when they see more souls saved. The Lord will send in people through the bus ministry where the whole family will eventually get saved because you picked up the children. This has been the case in hundreds of families and these folks become some of our finest workers in the churches.

Distance of Routes

Twelve buses at the Highland Park Baptist Church only travel a distance of approximately 8 to 10 miles from the church; which means their greatest concentration of people come from a short distance from the church. Two of their buses, according to Dr. Faulkner, travel a distance of up to 20 miles from the church. Dr. Jack Hyles runs some of his buses as much as 30 to 80 miles away from the church. The longer bus routes that he is running are involved in what is called a "B" Sunday school. The buses pick up the children so that they actually miss the ordinary Sunday school classes but arrive at the church in time to go into the Junior churches and the morning church services. After the morning service is over the regular folks and most of the buses leave but the "B" Sunday school then begins and lasts for some 45 minutes and then they who have traveled the longer distance travel to their homes.

In Trinity Baptist Church of Jacksonville, Florida, approximately 30 to 35 miles would be the longest distance *one way* that a bus would ride. Some of the most successful routes that we had were in the Jacksonville Beach area and had to cross one toll bridge and a river that was over a mile wide at that particular spot and buck the beach traffic in order to get to the westside location of our church. (This route was started after we erased from our mind the idea that the bus ministry was simply a matter of transportation.)

Many buses racked up as much as a hundred miles on the round trip from the church going out to pick up the children and back to the church. This means that their total running for just the Sunday morning activities if they started at the church would be 200 miles. I feel it would be best for anyone just starting a bus ministry to keep the mileage within approximately 15 miles of the church to start with as it may make your bus ministry a real problem until you get in gear. Some have often asked how many people were running buses in the Jacksonville area. We had a city that was loaded with at least 60 or more church buses running down the various streets. Some of the areas that our bus captains worked were also being worked by as many as six other church buses coming down the same streets knocking at the same doors. Sometimes there are mistakes in getting on the wrong bus and ending up at the wrong church. We have had very successful routes where three or four other buses were running from other churches in the same area.

Dr. Bob Gray said, "If anyone gets killed in Jacksonville it will probably be because he was run over by a church bus!" We had a neighboring church in Jacksonville that was eight blocks away which was also operating a great number of church buses and several other churches in the immediate area that were fundamental that were running the same neighborhoods as our buses. The best, of course, is to find a prospective area where no one is working so that there will not be a sense of competition involved.   I did not say *where no church was* but rather *where no buses* are running.

It is perfectly all right also to go into an area where others are already running buses. People will soon learn whether the bus captain and people involved in your bus ministry have a real *heart* for the neighborhood and they will ride the bus where the people are the most interested spiritually and sincerely in them.

I have mentioned several of the types of prospect areas — trailer courts, housing projects, slum areas, apartment buildings, and so forth. *Now, settle on an area, not too large, and start working the area.* In a later chapter on visitation I will tell you exactly what to say and how to make each call.

There are several ways that people count their attendance on the buses. Some encourage all of their *members* to ride the bus even though they would normally come in a car. Some folks will do this to save gasoline. Others count their bus attendance made up of the workers who ride the bus (which could number five or six) and the kids. Others just count the bus driver, captain, and his family, and the children. It would be wise to set a policy of *how* to count the buses to start with.

2. SECURE A BUS

In Jim Lyons' wonderful lecture on the bus ministry given at the Pastors' Conference in Hammond, Indiana, in 1965, he mentions his first point as being, "*Get a bus.*" Although this is rather elementary, it is nonetheless something of an important thing to accomplish. Our church spent in Jacksonville approximately $1,000.00 per month on bus rentals alone. This does not include several hundred dollars we spent for repairs, insurance, gasoline, etc., on our own buses that we owned. It also did not include the purchasing of new equipment. The approximate cost of a bus depends, of course, on the area in which you live, the condition of the buses, and the demand for them. In our area (the Jacksonville, Florida, area), the county does not own the buses that are run for the schools but there are local contractors who contract to the public schools and run the buses for a fee. This is a wonderful situation for a church in that they don't have to maintain and insure a great fleet of buses. Although we operated 17 buses on Sunday, only four of those were actually our own. We owned four of them so that we could have parties for the young people's groups and field trips for our Christian school and occasionally Sunday school classes used the buses for outings. There is always a use for one or two buses. I would suggest that if possible it would be wise to rent the buses as a whole rather than pay all of the upkeep, etc. (There is one thing that I learned about the bus ministry, and that is that I haven't learned anything about the bus ministry. What I am saying is that a lot of these things will be only applicable to one area or to one situation. You must find out what will work best for your own church. If you have a number of good mechanics in your church and have found a very reasonable source of buses it could be the best thing in the world to develop a large bus fleet of your very own that you could run Sunday morning, Sunday night, and Wednesday night, and for your revivals.)

We rented our buses at a mileage rate for the most part. Some of the buses ran for a flat rate of $15, $20, or $30 for one run. This would include paying the driver, buying the gas, and the use of the bus which is insured at the owner's expense. This would allow them to drive from the place where the bus is kept, making the route, coming to the church, and then return driving all of the route and back home for this amount of $15, etc. In Lynchburg, Virginia, Dr. Falwell rented city buses for a flat rate by the hour ($17 for each Sunday morning). This was figuring a two-hour run for the buses. They would start at the bus barn, meet the bus captain there, run with the city bus driver the entire route and let the children off at the church. The bus would go back to the barn and the bus driver would then meet the people in front of the church at the time the service was over. Since Dr. Falwell's service was on television he was very punctual about letting the church service out and therefore the bus drivers knew exactly when to be there. (Sometimes, some churches have been able to work with a bus contractor where someone in their church who has a chauffeur's license will drive the bus for nothing for the church and this reduces the cost of the bus by about $5.00 per week.)

Other than a flat rate fee for the buses we have paid the following to our bus drivers for some time. Ten dollars for the first 20 miles and 35 cents per mile for every mile after that. This, in some cases, amounts to $15 and in other cases amounts to $20 or $30 for one bus route. This is paid to the bus contractor who also normally was the driver who drove the bus. (Some of the contractors hire their drivers and do not run the routes themselves and give the drivers $5.00 or sometimes a percentage of one-third of the money taken in for the trip.)

We have found that when you own the bus yourself it usually will still cost you between $15 and $20 per week even though you furnish your own driver, free. As I mentioned before, sometimes this can be greatly reduced by the type of equipment you own, the ability of your people to work on the buses, and the length of the routes, etc. Some churches have been able to secure a bus for a flat rate of, for instance, $10 per week. This would include all of the services on Sunday morning, Sunday night, and Wednesday night. The church would furnish their own driver and gasoline. In each case you will have to find out how much the buses would rent for in your area if you're going the *rental route*.

I do believe you should run your buses each service of the church. There may be a situation where you will have to combine two or three routes into one bus for the evening or Wednesday night runs. We have found in our church that when we teach faithfulness to the people and then do not run the buses we are becoming inconsistent to what we're teaching. Usually the evening bus crowd is not quite as great but will enhance the services by having many unsaved people there. We have, for instance, a great number of Catholic children who ride our buses on Sunday night and Wednesday night but go to the Catholic Sunday school on Sunday morning. We would not be able to reach them if we did not run the buses on Sunday night and Wednesday night. Rev. Zeno Groce, Woodland Baptist Church, Winston-Salem, North Carolina, has as big or a bigger crowd on his Wednesday night and Sunday night bus runs than on Sunday morning. He has purchased his own buses and spotlessly painted them inside and out. He even laid indoor-outdoor carpet on the floor of each bus and provided additional take-out steps for the older people as some buses have a rather large first step. His buses bring in three to four hundred in the evening services of the church.

It may be in your area that there are no rental buses but the county owns all of the buses themselves and will not rent them. There may be no reasonable way to rent a city bus or secure use of one from a transportation company. In this case you will probably have to buy all of the buses you will run on your routes. Allow me to inject here several paragraphs on how to buy a bus. I have purchased a great number of buses for the churches that I have worked in, plus purchased buses for those in which I have set up their bus ministry.

What Size?

I suggest that the buses you purchase would be the ones that *seat the most*. In this age of demonstrations I would have to carry a large placard that would say, "*BAN THE VAN*." I would *not* suggest that you buy a 24-passenger bus but rather that you would try to get the largest possible one. The usual size is the 66-passenger although they do make 72 and 75-passenger buses. Some of the pusher bus types carry from 55 to 75 passengers. Some of these are very high in their initial cost and others of the rear-engine type have such costly motors that they would be impractical for most churches.

There are many reasons for getting a larger bus. One is the psychology of it. If a man has a challenge of filling a van that holds 12 people and he fills it he thinks he has done a tremendous job! If you challenge him with a 60-passenger bus he still looks for that 60 to be filled. Very frankly, it's just as easy to pack a 60-passenger bus as it is a 12-passenger bus. Therefore, why stifle the initiative of some good bus captain with a small vehicle so that he feels he has completed his job. This is much like building a church building that seats only 100 people. When you get to 125 in that building it will drop back to about 80 and then back to 125 and then back to 80. The people will not come in the crowded circumstance and until you build larger, you will not expand.

Another reason for the large bus is that it costs just

about the same to operate a 66-passenger bus as it does a 24 or 30-passenger bus. The ratio of price regarding a van and a large bus usually amounts to the fact that the van is far *more* expensive than the large bus. Excellent used buses may be secured at three to five hundred dollars. There are very few vans that are fit to run that could be purchased for this price. (A van meaning one of the small 9 to 12-passenger series of vehicles put out by, for instance, the Econ-O-Line, Ford, Chevrolet, Dodge Van, etc.) The total potential of your bus fleet can only be measured in your capacity of the buses. Therefore, if you have five vans with a total capacity of 60 people then you are involving five of your fine workers and their time in getting only 60 people. Would it not be much better to have five 60-passenger buses to bring in 300 with the same five workers? Remember, every time you add a bus you add the potential of the total amount of seating capacity on that bus to your attendance.

What Shape?

Look for a bus that has a *good body* on it—one where there are not many glasses broken out, where there is not a great deal of rust (which is usually evident around the back door of the bus and the front door of the bus or the front fenders of the bus). Again there may be some variance here as to what would suit your situation. You may have someone in your church who owns a body shop and has a lot of time and would like to spend that time fixing a bus up and painting it. If so, and they will do it for nothing, of course, this is the thing to do. You also may have someone who is very mechanically inclined and may have a source of used engines and transmissions. Therefore, it would be an easy matter for you to fix up a bus that would be considered a "junker" to others. You will have to adapt each one of the things I say to your own situation. Basically, we look for the good body rather than the good motor... the reason being, it is easier to replace a motor or transmission with another used motor or transmission than to get all new glass, seats, a new body, or to fill and sand all kinds of rust holes and sheet metal work. It costs approximately $140.00 or more to paint a bus of the school bus size, therefore, if the paint is in good shape it is also helpful. (In some states the counties will not allow you to take a bus on the road unless the school bus paint colors have been painted out. This is true now in the state of Florida. A bus must be identified other than the chrome yellow of the normal school bus before it will pass the state safety inspection. Check on this with your State Highway Patrol before you purchase a bus so that it will not cost you a great deal of money to repaint or to change something on the bus.) There are many dollars' worth of glass in a bus and so you should look to see if all the glass is in the bus. The seats, although maybe not the best, can sometimes be fixed up with some tape and reupholstered by some of the people in the church. However, it is best to find a bus body that is in fairly good shape and the motor and transmission ready to go. In other words, it would probably *not be best* to buy one without a motor for $150.00 and put in a lot of parts and a lot of labor. It would more than likely be to your advantage to purchase one for approximately $400-$500 that is in good shape. You may have willing men that will give much of their free time to work on a bus and make repairs. However, it would be better to buy the more expensive bus and put the willing men to work on the bus routes *to fill the bus!*

It is best to try to find the bus that ran last year on the school route. Most of these buses had to meet certain standards. I have bought buses in the state of New York where the buses are pulled in every six months and the brake linings, lights, motors, exhaust systems, glass, are all checked along with the tires and other items. Therefore, if you buy one of these buses it will more than likely be in very good running condition. (Some states have more stringent inspections than others.) But note, be sure to make your vision large enough when you think of your bus ministry. You may be thinking in terms of purchasing one bus and then filling it and then purchasing a second bus and filling it, etc. You will find out as you start the bus ministry that it is wise to buy buses in multiples. If you can, always have one to use for a spare and as a challenge to someone else in the church constantly to take another route. When all your buses are used, buy another bus by faith and get ready to start another route.

Where?

Some independent bus contractors will phase out their equipment and will possibly be interested in selling it direct rather than trading it in to a bus dealer. You can find these buses usually parked beside houses and ask them where the contractor is who owns the bus. You could call the county schools and find out who owns the buses and get a list from them of the bus contractors. Also, there may be lodges or fraternal orders that have purchased buses in the past and find there is not much use for them and would be interested in selling them. The county school buses and county school bus garages are great sources of buying buses on a *bid* basis.

Some cities have people who are in the bus chartering business and will be retiring certain vehicles. Also there is the possibility of finding a city bus line that is going out of business or is retiring some of their equipment. Sometimes they may own two or three school buses and are not interested in keeping them any more. (Again let me mention that it is probably better for most people to purchase the school-bus type of vehicle that has the *engine in the front*—one that could be purchased more readily such as a Ford or Chevrolet, instead of a more difficult and rarer type of bus, such as a Reo, White, etc. Some of these latter buses have excellent engines but the parts run very high and sometimes are difficult to come by.) Again, it is usually not to the best interest of the church to purchase a city-bus type vehicle. This is the kind with the two doors in the side and the rear engine, airbrakes, etc. The parts for these are quite costly and they are very well used vehicles. It is rather like buying a taxi cab in preference to the little old lady's car.

Most bus contractors keep their buses for about nine or ten years, then will depreciate them out on their income tax and have them for sale. They will then try to trade them in to the folks from which they are purchasing new buses. It seems as though I never pass a bus that is sitting somewhere that I don't wonder if it is for sale and how much it would cost. The other day I saw one several blocks down the street and was just about to get in my car and find out how much it would cost (I was in a strange town) when the bus moved on down the road and I saw it had some children in it being taken home from school.

Looking in the yellow pages in your phone book will probably reveal any of the bus *dealers* in your city or in adjacent cities. These will be people who deal mostly in new bus bodies and would have some access to used buses or possibly trade-ins. I never try to pay first price but always try to dicker with them to get them down to the price of the buses. We can save much money for the Lord that way. You may have to go to an adjacent state to find good buses.

In the state of Florida the demand for buses is great because of the outdoor camping craze and the fact that many folks are making campers out of them. Additionally, we have a great migrant worker population and this holds the price of buses quite high. Used buses that have been used by the migrants are almost impossible to use on church runs (they are usually worn out and torn up). It is best to find an area that might be considered remote where no one is particularly interested in buses or near some large city where they have hundreds of buses in the school system and not much of a market for selling them. One can buy a good used bus for anywhere from $150.00 on up into the thousands.

3. THE KEY, THE BUS CAPTAIN

"And I sought for a man among them, that should make up the hedge, and stand in the gap before me for the land, that I should not destroy it: but I found none." — Ezek. 22:30.

I suppose the most frequently asked question I run into in setting up bus ministries and advising those who already have them set up is, "What kind of a person is a bus captain?" You can advertise in the newspaper, announce it on the radio, put out mailers and fliers, ride through the streets with a public address system, and let everyone know that you are going to have a bus ministry. But you may run your buses up and down every street in town and they will come back to the church empty. The reason is that all of these things will only give a limited interest scope to your ministry. The most important person in your bus ministry setup is the bus captain himself. His route and the entire bus ministry rises or falls on who you have for bus captains. Yes, the key to the church bus ministry is the bus captain. There may be hundreds of pastors reading this book who have many "Preston Morrises" who are just waiting to be trained and turned loose to bring in thousands of people into fundamental churches.

Captains or Pastors?

Dr. Lee Roberson at the Highland Park Baptist Church in Chattanooga, Tennessee, calls his bus captains, "pastors." The majority of these folks are studying for the ministry in Tennessee Temple Schools and this is a definite training period for them. Because a number of people have patterned their ministries after Dr. Roberson they also have called the bus captains "pastors." In his situation it works perfectly well. I have found, however, that you must tailor the name of the individual who runs the bus route to your particular circumstance. We had originally, at Trinity Baptist Church, Jacksonville, Florida, called our bus captains, "pastors." This seemed like a good idea except there were several men of the church who felt that because they were called "pastors" they should meet pastoral requirements. (Husband of one wife, children in subjection, etc.) Therefore, they felt a woman could not be the husband of one wife and therefore would not be eligible to be a bus captain. In a very real sense of the word there are not *many* pastors of the bus routes. The pastor of the church is pastor of the bus routes as well as everything else that is connected with the church. Otherwise a situation could arise where one bus captain who brings in seventy or eighty could decide that one week he would start a new church with his seventy or eighty because he is the pastor of them and does not agree with the pastor of the main church. *The bus captain* is a person who goes into a neighborhood or area and brings people physically to the church where the pastor of the church then ministers to them.

There are some churches that pay their bus captains a salary (again, Dr. Roberson does his students) but on the whole it seems it works much better with volunteer labor except for some very few exceptions (where there is a school in connection with the church). Also, it has worked quite well to use ladies as bus captains. Dr. Jack Hyles in Hammond, Indiana, brings in some 2,000 on seventy-some buses with many of his bus captains being ladies.

The Thomas Road Baptist Church in Lynchburg, Virginia, has a number of lady bus captains. Some months ago I set up this bus ministry for Dr. Jerry Falwell and noted recently that one of their female bus captains, Carolyn Harris (who is just 15 years old), had 91 on her bus on one Sunday. They have recently had over 800 on buses alone for one Sunday in *the first year* of their bus ministry. (They are averaging 700 per Sunday on buses.)

Getting the Key

Dr. Jack Hyles suggests that people who respond to the invitation given by the pastor concerning soul winning be channeled to buses in order to give this dedication vent. This is a tremendous idea and should be followed in many churches. Normally, I require a bus captain to go with another captain for several weeks before they are put on their own. In some cases this does not have to be done. I ask them to promise me, the Lord, and the people of the church that they will visit three hours faithfully every week on their bus route. (Many visit many more hours than this.) When you start multiplying this by the number of bus routes you have, you find that there is a tremendous amount of visitation going on in your area and a saturation process for almost every home.

It is best to have two bus captains per route. Then it is not quite so easy to get discouraged about going on visitation or about the weather that is involved on the visitation day.

One Saturday it was pouring down rain and a lady who lives with her mother noticed her mother go to the door and look down the street. Her mother made the statement, "Who is that fool going door-to-door in the rain?" The lady went to the door to see such a sight and said, "That's no fool, Mother, that's Brother Beebe visiting on the bus route." (The best day for visitation by bus captains seems to be Saturday when the parents and children are home together.) When you have two bus captains, the one, if he is a man, can drive the bus and the other can run up to the house and knock on the door and help the children out to the bus.

Another way of securing bus captains would be to talk to your people who come into the church by letter immediately about helping you out on one of the bus routes visiting with another captain. Then ask him to pray about this ministry and whether he would like to take a route himself if he were trained. Usually when a person comes into the church he is not burdened with other activities such as teaching Sunday school, or Training Union class, etc. I feel it wise to loose the bus captain from all other responsibilities so he may concentrate his efforts on the bus route.

Additionally, the bus captain goes on soul-winning visitation on whatever day you have it in your church. He then takes the unsaved prospects he has run into on Saturday and follows them up with soul winning in mind. Good bus captains will make a good bus ministry in your church. Once they get into the habit of visiting three hours a week and see the basic way to visit and approach the people on the route they will be able to utilize this time to a great advantage and will consistently and constantly be bringing new people on their buses every single week.

When a route gets to fifty or sixty constantly then it is time to try to find someone to take part of this route and split the route because in just a few weeks that same route will be doubling itself if two captains are working in two separate directions.

Strange Creatures

What kind of strange creatures are bus captains? Bus captains come in all sizes and shapes and forms. From Becky Cash who is 17 years old and had 22 on the route her first Sunday to 15-year-old Carolyn Harris who came in with 91 on one Sunday to little old ladies who live on farms. Without going into detail let me describe some of the people and occupations.

I had one bus captain who was a driver for a large trucking company. He was one of the finest bus captains I ever had and yet he would get discouraged and every few months would want to quit. (I said that to encourage you. Even the best will want to quit sometimes.)

I had another bus captain that was a ladies' hairdresser and he was a fine captain.

I had another bus captain that I could never remember seeing him wear a tie. He was constantly putting up stovepipe and moving people on his route and was always bringing in great numbers.

I recall one fine bus captain, who although a prince of a man, was not a real outgoing personality. This man was a bachelor and consistently brought in tremendous numbers on his route and won souls constantly. He was not a person that was noted for a gift of gab and yet God used him in this ministry tremendously.

I am thinking of another bus captain that was very dear to my heart and we had good fellowship together. This man had an extremely homey way about him and was a very outgoing personality and would make himself completely at home in each situation.

I have bus captains that could hardly talk in saying more than two or three sentences. I have had others who were extremely wordy. It makes no difference, God can take all kinds of personalities and use them to gain people for His glory in the bus ministry.

4. ADDITIONAL HELP

It is wise if you have a larger church to put a good man in charge of all the bus captains that you intend to have. If you are launching, for instance, four or five buses it would be wise to have one man who does not go on the route, other than to visit with the other captains, as the man in charge. Perhaps your assistant pastor or music director would be good in this regard or another man who is very responsible in the church. In smaller churches, of course, the pastor would have to take this responsibility to be in charge of all the routes. I feel it wise for the bus captains to be responsible to someone who is a full-time staff member.

I also ask for a *secretary* on each bus. This could be a man or a woman who will help by checking the attendance which I will explain when I print later in the booklet a picture of the bus attendance cards. They also can make out the welcome badges or the triplicate forms that can be used to identify the children. Also they can give out any candy treat as the children leave the bus so that the last thing the children remember from Sunday school is the sweet treat. This person could be a teen-ager or it could be the wife of one of the bus captains or the bus driver's wife.

I believe that the pastor, or whoever is in charge of the bus captains, should feel very close to these men and should try to help them personally with all of their problems as much as possible. I will mention later on about how the visitation is done and how I go and visit with the bus captain, talking over their problems with them as I go. I am probably closer to the bus captains in our church than any other group of the people. We are constantly sharing the problems of the people on the routes where they are asking advice. Often I make visits for them and try to win the parents of the children, etc.

Our qualifications of the bus captains are rather general in a way. We do not have any bus captain who uses tobacco in any form nor is worldly, attending the theatre or movies, or drinks, or anything that would be questionable at all in the Christian life. Naturally, the bus captain must be saved and a good member of the church. (There are some churches who do not make such stringent requirements of their bus captains and allow many different folks to pick up people and to run their buses. Again, whatever you feel led to do in this regard would be the rule of thumb.) Several of our bus captains also happen to be deacons in our church. These men should be above reproach because they do a lot of visitation and represent the people of the church to the people. They must be extremely loyal as they control a good number of children and people and their opinions about the pastor would soon be known. Many of these folks will receive a crown much larger than even some full-time pastors because of their concern and burden for the lost.

In reading over some of the visitation for last week, I noticed that one captain had visited eight hours on his bus route and eight hours the week before. This man received absolutely no pay for this and he used his own car and gasoline to make the visits. Also, of course, he used his own free time for this. I know that God will give him a great crown and also to all of these bus captains who have such a great share in winning the lost for Christ. Select good captains and pray for them constantly.

5. POLICY

By way of information, the driver of the bus is usually never the best captain. (Some good churches practice the opposite of this and the captain is *always* the driver.) The driver should start blowing the horn as he approaches the stop where the child lives and if the child does not come out the bus captain should run up to the door and knock on the door until the parents get up and come to the door. Believe me, they will have the child ready for next week. Some bus captains make the mistake of leaving too soon because the child is not seen there at the door. I have had the experience of leaving some that were in the bedroom combing their hair or making final adjustments on their clothing. If you leave one it will take months to get that one back. Make sure that they are either not at home or completely not ready to go. Some have mentioned that honking the horn might get them arrested early on Sunday morning but we have never had this occasion arise and the ones who did this had the largest routes. (No driver should ever leave the bus running to get out and give assistance to a stalled motorist or to go to the door. This is why it is best to have two people on the bus that are responsible adults.) The bus captain, because he is not the driver, can be free then to do what is needed on the bus, keep order on the bus and to make sure that everyone is in proper discipline. Another tip is to never back the bus up into a parking space, the church parking lot, or a street unless a responsible adult is behind the bus in the full view of the driver through the rear view mirror directing him. We have several buses that have backed into parked cars or cars that had pulled too close behind the bus. Another reason why the bus driver would not be the best bus captain is that the captain can keep order on the bus and attend to the needs of the children that are being picked up.

A word about the Sunday pickup. On Saturday the bus captain advises the parents as to what time they will be by to pick up the children. It would be wise for your church to print up a small piece of card stock usually eight or nine inches long and about three inches wide with a hole cut in the top with a slit at the top that can be hung on a door. These are called "door-hangers." Ours has a picture of a bus at the top and says, "Your bus captain was by. Sorry I missed you. We will be by for the children at ———————— Sunday morning. Thank you for letting them come! Your bus captain's name is ————. Your bus captain's phone number is ————. First Baptist Church, Ruskin, Florida, Wally Beebe, Pastor, 645-1796." The bus captain can in advance fill in his name and telephone number. He can have a number of these in his pocket and if the people are not home, whether they be regulars or absentees, he can hang this "door-hanger" on the knob and simply fill in the time that his bus will be by on that route. By this the parents know that the captain has been faithful to come by and visit and the piece of literature counts to them as a visit and personal contact.

On Sunday morning, the bus captain meets the bus somewhere on his route and leaves his car at a gas station, in a parking lot, on a street, or in the church parking lot. He then rides with the bus driver and the bus to the first pickup. My bus captains are required to keep a record of what time they make their first pickup so that I know how long the children have to ride the bus and if they are late I know what time they started picking up the children. This helps me in analyzing the problems they have when they are late. Usually our bus captains start at 8:30 picking up the buses and starting their routes. They are usually concluded between 9:30 and 9:45 which is when Sunday school starts. It is advisable not to get the children there too early as they should not have to wait around for twenty minutes before the Sunday school teachers and staff arrive. They can get into much too much mischief during this time.

Chapter 4

Implementation

We have now studied *why* we should have a bus ministry and some of the preparation involved in starting the bus ministry. After I have secured a bus captain and a bus, I then take the bus captain and myself on a tour of the prospective areas that we are going to choose from; where we will start a route. We pray much about it and then just drive through an area looking for children and looking for signs that this is where the Lord would have us start a route. Now we will go step by step into the implementation of starting the bus route from scratch. We have a bus lined up for Sunday and a prospective area that we are going through which we have marked out on a map. We have a bus captain ready and so we will go visiting with the bus captain first of all. (In the front of the church I usually put a challenge board with the names of the bus captains and the number they had on their buses on Sunday. This helps the captain feel his sense of responsibility in that the Lord, the people of the church who purchased the bus, the pastor, and the children on the route are depending on him to keep the route up. On occasion I will point to one of the routes that is extremely high and joke about this captain trying to find how many people he can stuff into one 60-passenger bus, etc. (I had a captain recently put 121 on a 61-passenger bus!) The challenge boards can be simply the regular attendance boards with the title "Buses" or "Bus Routes" and the name of the people on each line.)

1. VISIT THE BUS ROUTE

Although some of our men work on Saturday who have bus routes, most of them do not. I ask each man who comes forward and says he would like to be a bus captain to call a minimum of *three hours per week*. These visits are usually made on Saturday. It is best to find both the children and the parents home when making the first approach to the neighborhood. If you find just the children at home they will say, "Well, I'll have to ask my parents." If you find just the parents at home they will say, "I'll ask the kids and find out if they would like to come." Hence, it is best to deal with both parents and children. I normally get penny candy or bubble gum to fill my pockets with when I go out on Saturday. When I knock at the door I start to talk to the mother about the children coming and usually a child will peek around from behind mother's skirts. As you are talking to the parent it is wise to reach in your pocket and pull out the penny candy and extend your hand towards the child. The child will reach out and receive the candy and almost always the mother will say, "What do you say to the man?" This, in a way, obligates the parent towards you and the parent thinks, "That man likes my child, I will let my child go with that man."

Sometimes visiting on the bus route must be done during the week or in other spare times. For instance, I had one man who worked in a bank and was off early every day and took about an hour or so and went visiting after his banking job in his area for the bus route. He also visits on Saturday.

Three hours is a minimum but not a maximum.

Sometimes there is more required than just this visitation to keep the bus route up. For instance, if a route drops down below the 30 mark I always feel it is in trouble and needs a great deal of prayer and help. This is where the head bus captain can come in and help the bus captain who is down. We usually have several routes in the 60's, several in the 50's, and the remainder in the 40's and 30's. In the back of the book you will find a Sunday's attendance described that was a normal Sunday.

Easy Canvass

Within a few more sentences we will be describing the different ways to visit a bus route but I first of all want to call your attention to the *easiest way*. You have no doubt heard of door-to-door canvassing and a block canvass, etc. The easy canvass is one in which you make no attempt to record who lives in every house on the block or area in which you are going. You simply drive through the area and look for children's signs around the house or children playing in the yard. These signs have been described previously. (Dirt around the door, toys in the yard, broken screens, tire swing, etc.) These are the easiest and quickest to pick up. These are the kind of homes that will fill your buses with prospects for salvation in no time at all. When you feel you have exhausted the easy ones then it is wise to go back and systematically, house by house and street by street, check off each home, finding out who lives there and also getting the prospects on the buses.

Several Basic Ways

There are many basic ways to gain prospects for the bus route. *The best way* is a *referred lead.* This means that you have a friend who has a friend on the bus route. This friend knows these people do not attend church and are lost and do not have a way to go and would be willing to attend. This, of course, is the best prospect you could possibly have as you go to the door knowing someone they know. This is a more friendly and cordial visit. Also you are in a rather sure-fire situation in that you know they have children and know that they want to attend. However, this is normally not the case with a bus route. If you can gain a large map of your county or city area where you run your routes you can color or shade in the area where each bus goes. Then put a key to the shading beside the map indicating the phone number and bus captain's name and address. Sometimes your people will run into other people on visitation who would make tremendous prospects and they can go to this map and then phone the bus captain this information. He can, on Saturday visitation, close the deal and line up the children for the route.

The next best prospect is to find *children playing in the yard* or in the street by the house. I always go over to the children and ask them if they attend Sunday school anywhere regularly. If they go to a *non*-fundamental church and go regularly, I try to ask them about their salvation experience and lead them to the Lord.

If they go to a fundamental church or express the fact that they attend even rather sparsely a fundamental church, I encourage them to go to that church and do not bother them any more. This is very important and God will not honor sheep-stealing just for the sake of numbers. (Or for any other sake.)

If, however, they do not say that they go to any church, then I ask for their address and go by to see their parents, usually taking the children and asking for permission to take them to Sunday school on the bus the following day. I try to win the confidence of the children on the way to the home so they will be really anxious to go.

The next best prospect would be an "*electrical cut-in card.*" This we secure from the *Financial News* which comes every day telling us everyone that gets their electricity turned on (in Jacksonville). You could do this through your water company, public utilities, gas company, or Chamber of Commerce. We have a listing of the streets on each route and one secretary takes these listings and puts the new "cut-ins" on cards and gives them to the bus captain as having moved in the previous week. They then go and call on them in the neighborhood telling them that they are happy they moved into the neighborhood and wonder if they have a church home yet, and could we bring their children on the bus?

[margin note: NEAT BUT OUT of DATE]

The next best prospect is the *block-canvassing,* where you just go, "cold turkey," door to door looking for prospects for the bus route. I will tell you what to say in these encounters in just a few moments. Let me mention why each one of these is decreasing in its efficiency in being a prospect. First of all, if you go canvassing just door to door, you do not know whether anyone is home and sometimes it takes several minutes to find out if the house is vacant or at least that the people are not in when you call. (You must think *TIME!* Since I believe that a person's time is extremely valuable I try to train my bus captains to pack in several more hours of conventional visitation into their three hours. Therefore, when they are making their routes they should be constantly thinking to themselves "time, time, time." They should be finding ways to cut down the time-factor and improve their efficiency.)

Secondly, you may call and find that the people are regular attenders at another church and are old established people in the neighborhood.

Thirdly, you may call and find that there is just one person who lives there who is possibly single and does not have any children and therefore you have no "in" with the Sunday school bus. Therefore you eliminate some of these problems with the electrical cut-in. An "electrical cut-in" is usually someone who has just moved into town. (By the way, maybe a "welcome wagon" list would also help you in this regard. It might be possible for you to get several members of your church who are in business to sponsor a "welcome wagon" lady to visit one half a day five days a week distributing tracts and information regarding the church and these businesses.) People who just move are easy to meet and would probably appreciate a visit from someone who wants to be friendly. However, you face the prospect of still finding someone who is single or still someone who is not interested in attending church or riding the bus. You may find a married couple that have no children and therefore again you are out of luck about the *bus approach*. (The bus approach is looking for kids.) This means that when you see children out on the street playing, you have a short cut to several things because first of all you know that they are there because you see them. Secondly, you know that they are children because of their age. The only problem then is whether they attend church or not.

Soul Winning Later

This may be a shocking sentence because we are all interested in winning souls and the bus ministry is soul winning personified. However, we are *not* interested in doing a great deal of soul winning on the bus routes because this would absorb a great deal of your time. Since you are thinking, "Time, time, time," you must make a great number of quantity calls and not quality calls. We are not trying to present every ministry of the church, the history of the pastor, etc. You are instead trying to make as brief a contact as possible and receive a committal for the people to come to church on the buses. Whenever the opportunity does present itself, whenever a child, teen-ager, or parent is alone, I usually with my partner try to lead this person to the Lord — if I see that this person is ready to accept the Lord and it would not take much time.

The Devil is extremely shrewd. As you visit your bus routes you may run into a Jewish rabbi, a Roman Catholic, Jehovah's Witness, or some other notably different religious person. The Devil would whisper in your ear, "They would really take notice of you at church if you brought that convert back with you." You then proceed to witness to this person for an hour and a half of your three-hour allotment visitation time and would probably not win them to Christ, when in the same length of time you could line up twenty or thirty children or adults to come, riding the bus, who are waiting for someone just to come and invite them. Of this group, a great percentage would be saved the very first Sunday they came. Hence there is a definite way in which you would visit, trying to win souls all along the route, encouraging discouraged Christians, etc., and ruin your bus route ministry. I make this policy that if the person is alone in the home, and does not have a house full of company, or a group of children around them nagging on them, then I deal with them about their souls. (Again if they are not of a radically different religious background that I see would take a great deal of time, I deal with them.) Also, you may find someone who is a good prospect for salvation but there is company or an unfavorable situation for soul winning. You should make note of all of these people and then on the soul-winning night of your church when you have visitation, go back and visit among your bus-route people picking out the good prospects that you have lined up on Saturday and visit them with only the purpose of soul winning in mind. This does not rob you of the time that you must take on

Saturday to build your route and still allows you to be the soul winner you ought to be.

When a bus captain's route gets low the head bus captain should visit the route with the bus captain and try to observe if there is some negative suggestion that they are using, if there is a personality problem, or wrong method involved. I am reminded of the time I stopped to get a sandwich in a certain state. The teenage son was helping his father in the restaurant and came over and asked me, "You don't want a cup of coffee, do you?" No, I did not want anything somebody told me I should not have. Therefore, when you talk to people about getting their children to come on the bus routes you should be shaking your head slightly with a "yes" motion to encourage "yes" answers. Psychology? Absolutely!

Sometimes a bus route is low just as a test from the Lord to see how persevering we will be. It is the job of the head bus captain to encourage, help, and suggest. For instance, I visited one man's route who is a very fine bus captain—one of our best and yet his route was going down. I do not say that this is the only reason it was going down, but I'm sure it is one of them; however, when we went visiting together I noticed that he would use one expression everytime he came to the door and talked to the people involved. (By the way, we try to visit the faithful people on the bus route as well as the absentees each time. Some bus captains only visit the absentees each week and then look for new ones the rest of the three hours. Others will visit everyone on the route each week and prospects too. I believe that this would probably be the best policy for those just starting out, to visit each person on the route each week. This keeps the personal contact with the parents and we usually give out, as I mentioned before, a piece of bubble gum or candy to each child on the Saturday visitation. The children will be looking forward to your visit if you give them a treat each time.)

This man said to several people before I stopped him, "Would you want us to bring the bus by?" Now this was said to people who were *already riding the bus* or had been prospects for some time. My mind raced ahead as to what was in their minds as they heard this expression. I had a picture of this man going to all the trouble of bringing that great big sixty-six passenger bus out of his way to come over and try to pick them up. To me it struck a note of *negative suggestion*. It was as though it were a great trouble and burden for him to come by with the bus for the people. This was not the case at all, however, because he was delighted to do this and it was his job! So I suggested that instead of signing off their conversation with, "Would you want us to bring the bus by?" I said, "We'll be by in the morning for the kids; we sure love them and appreciate you sending them!" The visual picture was now, we were coming by anyway and we wanted them so much to attend. This may not have been all the problem involved, but certainly I feel it was somewhat of a contributing factor.

Smile

When you talk to the people on the bus route make sure that you smile when you are asking them questions and nod your head when you want an assent. I might mention here that although I discourage soul winning on the routes by our bus captains, you'll win more people by accident on a bus route situation than you will if you decide to do visitation and try to get someone saved. Wherever there are people you will find souls.

When the bus captains start out on their Saturday visitation, I encourage them to visit the absentees first, the regulars second, and use the time in between or afterward to get new ones. We check on all the children between the stops along the street asking them if they are attending Sunday school anywhere. The bus captain is supplied by the church with gum or penny candy from a wholesale house. The church can purchase this candy inexpensively and have it at a central location at the church so that after services each time the bus captain can replenish his supply. He should probably use bubble gum on Saturday and penny candy on Sunday as the child gets off the bus. Make sure that the children do not open their candy on the bus. If they did they could smear up someone's new dress or mess up the bus.

Sample Visit for Regulars

Here is a sample of the "*Howdy*" and "*Sixty-Second Call*" for the regulars. We are talking to a person who has come regularly and you want to maintain the contact with them. This takes just a few seconds and if you will do it, it will keep them interested. Before you go to the door you look at your records which I will describe in a later chapter and see that three of the children have come but little Johnny did not come Sunday. You knock at the door and say approximately this:

"Hi there, Mrs. Jones! How are you doing today? We were so happy to see the kids coming Sunday on the bus. We sure missed Johnny Sunday. Was he sick?... Well I certainly hope that his finger gets better. By the way, did your husband get that job yet? We're certainly praying for you all and appreciate your letting your children come. Good-bye and we'll see you tomorrow morning! It will be about 9:10."

This little conversation took less than one minute and yet included in it two very personal things to the parents. First of all you mentioned the child named Johnny. The mother is thinking to herself, "That man sees hundreds of people and has forty to fifty children on that bus and yet missed my little Johnny. That man must love my Johnny." This goes back to the same thing we've been preaching all along that it is *personal interest.* This is what will get to the hearts of these parents. By watching your records and taking a real interest in the people you can win their confidence and their heart for Christ. (Ask God to give you a real love for the people on your bus route that you might sincerely and honestly have a deep compassion for them and their needs.)

Be prepared with a Testament, tracts, business cards if possible stating your church and who you represent. I have mentioned before the doorknob hangers that you can make up and print on your mimeograph machine or have printed in a print shop. I also developed a piece of literature for several churches, among them being the Thomas Road Baptist Church in Lynchburg, Virginia. This literature states on the front, "Your special invitation to ride the bus." Under that on the front page there is a picture of one of the church buses with people getting on it. In an inset there is a picture of the pastor, Dr. Jerry Falwell, where it labels him as the minister, there is a little word "to" and a picture of the sanctuary of the church, the name, the location, and the phone number underneath. In the first fold inside there is a picture of children and just above this the caption, "We love children!" and under the picture "Lots of them!" These words follow... "Hundreds of parents trust us with their children each week. Here is what we do first... our courteous bus captain will pick up your child at the door. The captain then takes the child directly to his or her class where friendly, competent teachers receive them."

There is a picture of the nursery children with two-year-olds and the workers are smiling and laughing, playing with the children. The caption underneath reads, "Even two-year-olds ride the bus!" The next fold

56

starts at the top by saying, "Next... the older children, three through five, all go to Sunday school and then stay in the same place for a special children's church service." There is a picture here of a class of three to five-year-olds. Caption under this, "This includes a snack Bible story, games, singing and many other activities." Under that there is another picture of children eating a snack. The next fold starts, "Then... the older children, six through twelve years old, have a junior church hour also after their Sunday school class. Sometimes it's a special guest."

Then there is a picture of the junior church in progress with the man leading it. The leaflet continues, "It could be a flannelgraph lesson." There is a picture of the junior church worker placing a flannelgraph picture on the board. The caption under this picture is, "By the junior church pastor. (Teacher)"

On the back page of this brochure we read this caption, "Finally... after church is over the bus captain gets every child back on the bus and brings the child back to your door." We then have a picture of all the children's church workers smiling and looking attentive. Caption under this, "Our primary and junior church workers are eager to serve your children. Won't you let them come? The church address, pastor, and phone number are on the front of this folder. Please call us and give the secretary your name and address and we will stop this Sunday for your children. (Big caption at the bottom) WE LOVE CHILDREN!" The final fold of this leaflet says, "Your bus captain's name is ———, bus captain's phone number is ———, the bus will be by at ——— Sunday morning. Thank you!"

Just a word about how you may use this. If the people say they do not go anywhere to church then you will follow up by whipping out something like this and saying, "Let me explain to you what we are doing."

57

FINALLY...

AFTER CHURCH IS OVER THE BUS CAPTAIN GETS EVERY CHILD BACK ON THE BUS AND BRINGS THE CHILD BACK TO YOUR DOOR.

OUR PRIMARY AND JUNIOR CHURCH WORKERS ARE EAGER TO SERVE YOUR CHILDREN. WON'T YOU LET THEM COME? THE CHURCH ADDRESS, PASTOR, AND PHONE ARE ON THE FRONT OF THIS FOLDER. PLEASE CALL US AND GIVE THE SECRETARY YOUR NAME AND ADDRESS AND WE WILL STOP THIS SUNDAY FOR YOUR CHILDREN.

WE LOVE CHILDREN!

YOUR BUS CAPTAIN'S NAME

IS

BUS CAPTAIN'S PHONE NUMBER IS

THE BUS WILL BE BY AT _____
SUNDAY MORNING.

THANK YOU!

Your

SPECIAL INVITATION

to

RIDE THE BUS

JERRY FALWELL
Minister

to

THOMAS ROAD BAPTIST CHURCH
Thomas Rd. at Perrymont Ave.
Lynchburg, Va.   Phone 239-9261

WE LOVE CHILDREN!

LOTS
OF
THEM!

HUNDREDS OF PARENTS TRUST US WITH THEIR CHILDREN EACH WEEK. HERE'S WHAT WE DO.

FIRST...

OUR COURTEOUS BUS CAPTAIN WILL PICK UP YOUR CHILD AT YOUR DOOR. THE CAPTAIN THEN TAKES THE CHILD DIRECTLY TO HIS OR HER CLASS WHERE FRIENDLY, COMPETENT TEACHERS RECEIVE THEM.

EVEN 2 YR. OLDS RIDE THE BUS!

NEXT...

THE OLDER CHILDREN 3-5 YRS. ALL GO TO SUNDAY SCHOOL AND THEN STAY IN THE SAME PLACE FOR A SPECIAL CHILDREN'S CHURCH SERVICE.

THIS INCLUDES A SNACK, BIBLE STORY, GAMES, SINGING AND MANY OTHER ACTIVITIES.

THEN...

THE OLDER CHILDREN 6-12 YRS. OLD HAVE A JUNIOR CHURCH HOUR ALSO AFTER THEIR SUNDAY SCHOOL CLASS. SOMETIMES IT'S A SPECIAL GUEST.

IT COULD BE A FLANNELGRAPH LESSON.

BY THE JUNIOR CHURCH PASTOR.

The people see the picture of a bus and get the point that the bus will pick up their children. They do not have a strange idea of what a bus is for. You are showing them a picture of it. There is also a picture of the pastor. He looks trustworthy and therefore they feel they know him. They have a picture of him. There is also a picture of the church building where they will be and the phone number in case there is an emergency. There are pictures of children in the folder and pictures of their teachers. This folder can be left in the hands of the people with the bus captain's name and phone number previously filled out. Then at the door all he has to do is fill out the time that they will be coming by on the bus for those children.

Sample Call for New Ones

(If you can memorize this one statement that I will now make and change the words to fit your church you can build a bus route rapidly.) You go to the door, put on a smile, knock on the door and when the person answers you say, "How do you do, I am Rev. Beebe from the Trinity Baptist Church; we run a Sunday school bus through here and wondered if you folks attend church or Sunday school anywhere regularly?" If the reply is, "No, we don't," you start with your explanation of what you are doing there and the fact of the bus coming by the door to pick up the children. You could then ask them the names and ages of the children and write them down. Then I would ask them, "Would you be so kind as to let them come this Sunday with us on the bus?"

Electrical Cut-In Call

Here is what you would say to someone that you knew had just moved into the area either through the electrical cut-in or other means. "How do you do, I'm Rev. Beebe from the Trinity Baptist Church. We run a Sunday school bus right past your door and wondered if you folks have a church home yet?" Then you would follow up the answer with the appropriate response. If they say they do not go anywhere I continue with, "Fine! How many children do you have?" (Their reply.) "That's wonderful! We just love children at our church and we would love to have them come tomorrow morning on the bus. Here's what we do; we pick the children up at ——— and then take them directly to their Sunday school class. If they are ——— (whatever ages you have in your children's churches) they will receive a little snack and possibly something to drink at the children's church and have a message on their own level for the church service hour. Then they will be placed on the bus by this bus captain right here (I point at the captain visiting with me) and brought directly back to your door about an hour after the service is over. In other words we will pick up your child at about ——— (time) and he will get back just as soon after the service as we can get him back. It will be approximately between 12:30 and 1:00. May we come by and pick up the (child or) children?"

I introduce the bus captain who is visiting with me and tell the mother that this is the man who is our bus captain and will be on the bus to take care of the children the next day. I tell them again, "Do not get on the bus unless this man is on the bus. He will be the one on the bus that will pick up the children and show them where to go."

I know there will be someone who will wonder why I say this. Here is the reason. We were driving around on one of the routes and saw three children playing on a vacant parking lot of a supermarket. I called out from the car, "Hey, do you kids go anywhere to Sunday school?"

They said, "No, we don't."

I pulled up the car and got out and talked to them briefly. From across the lot came two more children. These were between the ages of 7 and 12 years of age, five in all. Four of them, I found out were brothers and sisters. After asking them whether they wanted to come to Sunday school and getting them lined up, I dealt with them about their souls and found that none of them had been saved. I had the joy of leading them all to Christ there as they prayed and knelt together with the bus captain and myself on the parking lot and received Christ in their hearts. After dealing with them about the assurance of their salvation and asking them if they really meant what they had done, I then led them on to the matter of making public profession of faith the next day. I asked the four children where they lived. They pointed to a house across the street that was yellow. I asked them how many children were in the family? They said, "Fourteen!"

We then made arrangements to pick up these children the next day. I asked one other child where he lived and it was next door. I went to the house and made arrangements with some of his brothers to pick them up also. Our bus captain went by the next day to pick them up and, of course, they were to make public professions of faith. When he got to their house he found the mother was very disturbed because she thought she had already put them on our church bus only to find out one of our neighboring churches had picked them up on their bus and taken them to their Sunday school. We had this happen one time to our own buses in that eight children got on the wrong bus and they found they were headed to the wrong church. We turned the bus around and delivered them to their church and then brought our load to ours. We are glad to reciprocate with fundamental churches that are neighbors. Needless to say after this experience, we assured the mother we would be by and pick up the children and she said she would not let them get on any other bus except the one where our bus captain was.

Some other helps in describing the bus captain on visitation is that he should be folksy, interested in the people, genuinely so. He is to be alert to opportunities to win people to Christ and also alert to digging up new families.

Goals

I encourage our bus captains and myself to pray for a goal each week on each route. (We also pray for a total goal for all the buses each week.) For instance, let's say that a bus captain prays for fifty-five on his bus for Sunday. All Saturday he thinks and prays for this figure. He says to himself (in prayer) all day as he visits the route, "Lord, give me fifty-five on this route Sunday. Where are the fifty-five that could ride my bus?" He sets a goal for the new ones every week also. I ask our bus captains to set a goal of at least *ten* new children lined up to come per week. (In Jacksonville we had a tremendous number of folks who moved away each week off of each route. We have had as many as twenty regular people move off a route on a given week end, on one bus.) In setting this goal he is talking about how many new ones he can get signed up on a Saturday visitation day who promise to come on Sunday.

There is a fall-out problem that you must face in this work. You may line up ten new ones in a week and very likely only two of these new ones will come. You might get discouraged and throw up your hands at this percentage but think it through. If you took the challenge, as many hundreds of people do with the bus ministry, and asked God to give you ten new ones each week, if only two of them came each week that would be one hundred in the course of a year. (Sit down right now and ask yourself an honest question as to how many people who *do not attend any church anywhere* live in the radius of your bus route. Surely then each week of the year you could line up ten of these people who would say, "Yes, I will come on Sunday.")

All day long the bus captain looks for the ten new ones that he is asking the Lord to give him. He prays, "Lord, give me ten new ones. Are some of these children some of the ten? Please give me ten new ones, Lord, for this coming Sunday." All of the bus ministry, of course, is predicated by prayer on the part of each one of the bus captains and all involved in the church. The setting of goals and praying for these things along with saying these things to yourself as you go is simply believing God and claiming His promises. It is wise for the bus captain to make a prayer list of some of the special parents on the route who need to be saved and to weekly go over the records of his route in prayer for these people. The head bus captain and pastor should pray for his bus captains each day and the captains pray for the pastor and head bus captain each day in turn.

2. CONTESTS

The contests that can be run on the bus routes fall into two categories. The first is a contest that rewards the children on the route for their bringing certain people or a certain number. The second is the contest that rewards the bus captain himself for getting his bus ahead as far as the new riders, increase in attendance or some other goal. In a contest, sometimes it is wise to use a *percentage of increase* of one bus over their last year's attendance in that they compete with themselves and come up with a percentage. (This makes it hard for those who are running a good attendance now to win.)

Some weeks ago we started using a contest based on *new visitors only*. In other words, most of the recent contests have been based on people who brought only new visitors who have never ridden the bus before. (Sometimes in a small church or smaller area you could say that a visitor would be someone who has never come to the church or someone who has not been in the past four months or three months or whatever you would establish as a gauge.)

Let us first talk about the contest that involves the children and rewards them.

Contests for Kids

Some contests will work in some places where they will not work in others. An example of this is when I listened to Jim Lyons' tape on the bus ministry and heard described an airplane contest I wanted to try. In this contest, everyone who brought ten visitors in a certain number of weeks received a free airplane ride. I promptly called up all the charter plane services and found out the rates of all types of aircraft. Then I figured out how much it would cost to charter a plane for a certain date after the contest. I had a big 40-passenger Convair airplane all chartered and ready to fly over Jacksonville for a 15-minute tour. After drawing pictures of the airplane and printing them on cards and sending them to all of the people riding the buses I found that the children were only slightly interested in the contest. As the contest went on, I found that there was a great reluctancy on the part of the children to bring many people and if they did, they expressed a desire that they did not want to ride in the plane if they won the contest. For some strange reason, they were *scared to death* of riding in an airplane and had no interest in it what-so-ever.

Instead of ordering them a hundred-dollar plane trip,

I ordered them a $2.00 Bible and had them work like dogs for it. They wanted the Bible for some reason more than the plane trip. You may live in an area, however, where your ordering a plane trip would be the greatest, most momentous occasion of their lives.

In a moment I will mention some of the church-wide contests that we used for buses and the people who ride them but for now let me mention a few of the individual contests just run by *one* of the bus captains.

One bus captain had a "treasure hunt." You could announce this one week in advance. (Or you could tell them that once a month you would do this but you would not tell them which Sunday it was so they must come every Sunday to get in on it.) You could tell them when they got back on the bus, after Sunday school was over and church was out, someone would be sitting right over a silver dollar (or paper dollar). The one who was sitting in the lucky seat got to keep the dollar as his very own.

Some of our bus captains have given away parakeets, baby rabbits, chickens, goldfish in plastic bags, yoyos, and kites.

I remember one Sunday we had a "kite" Sunday. Every child who brought a first-time visitor received a free kite and ball of string plus their visitors received a kite and ball of string. This was operated throughout the entire Sunday school. It happened that one of our bus captains was gone on vacation that week and we had a substitute captain who was keeping order on the bus. I had just made an announcement to the entire congregation that the bus children would receive their kites from their bus captain on the bus.

One of the children misunderstood my announcement and started to talk to the bus captain on the bus about getting his kite. The substitute bus captain, trying to keep order, told the child, "Sit down on that seat and

I don't want to hear another word from you or you won't get your kite!"

When this captain had finished the run and had this one little boy left he said to the boy, "Where do you live?" The boy said, "I kept trying to tell you, I don't ride this bus, I just wanted to get my kite."

The young man's parents were still waiting at the church at three o'clock when the nervous bus captain brought the child back. He did get his kite!

There are some ball point pens that may be purchased as low as four cents apiece and there are all kinds of bookmarks, pencils, wall mottoes and other things that would make excellent prizes for small contests on the buses.

One time we took a picture of the pastor and his family and gave that away to everyone who attended that Sunday on the buses. Another occasion we had pictures taken of everybody who attended and these pictures were printed up and given to the children the following Sunday. These were not photographs but rather we took the one photograph and had them printed on a white glossy piece of paper and gave these to the children. This is the photograph that you see on the front of the bus book. The children could pick out their very own picture in the large picture and of course, this was very interesting to them.

I know of one pastor who has used very effectively the small, inexpensive items such as the creepy crawlers, plastic baseballs, boats, American flags, or other novelty items. On a patriotic Sunday, the bus captains at Trinity, under the direction of Rev. Lenny Willinger, gave out little American flags to everyone who attended. During their visitation the week before they wore straw hats with patriotic bands around them. (It is possible to get these from novelty houses and also from car dealers or others who have promotions. Sometimes stores and groceries will have this too. Watch their promotions and use them for your own contest after they are through with them.)

Contests for Captains

<u>We would always try to run contests during hard Sunday school months for the buses or the bus captains especially. These contests would involve the bus captains working against each other.</u> We would usually use the first-time visitor numbers as the way to compute the winner. Sometimes we have used as a prize a set of commentaries, a Scofield Reference Bible, a tape recorder and several reels of tape. One of the best that we have ever found was a free trip to the Bahama Islands to visit one of our missionaries for the bus captain and his wife. We did this for a couple of years and then changed the trip to the land of Nicaragua, Central America, to visit another missionary that we had there. I would suggest a contest like this be stretched out over the entire summer. There are normally twelve to fourteen weeks in the summer depending on the way you look at the week. If you take a small amount for promotion out of every week's offering and set it aside for the bus contest promotion, it is quite easy to finance such a contest. It cost approximately $250.00 for us to send one bus captain and his wife to the Bahamas by plane and also give them over $100.00 spending money to take care of their needs while there. By the way, this is usually best to do when you have more than four or five bus captains. Till you do, it may not be a good idea to offer such a large prize. (Jack Hyles in a general contest to bring visitors offered a free trip to the Holy Land!) A second prize in this contest could be a free trip to a near-by Bible conference such as the Southwide Baptist Fellowship or some other conference that you know about.

These contests usually gain many hundreds of visitors

coming on the routes. Of course, many found Christ as their Saviour and also then the parents were saved and the whole family brought to the Lord. I think it is not a good idea to run a Sunday school contest *and* a bus contest at the same time. It is possible that one would like to have a Sunday school contest one portion of the year and a bus contest at a time of the year when it is usually hard to get attendance.

We have given away Bibles, New Testaments, bicycles, transistor radios, and all manner of things in bus and Sunday school contests.

3. KEEPING RECORDS

Any person who wants to be honest will keep good records. It is one thing to say, "Oh, we had a great number on our buses." It is another thing to say exactly how many you did have. It is also good for you to look back on the previous year and find out exactly how much you have grown or not grown on your bus ministry. Therefore, I keep records of every bus captain, his hour of departure, and his hour of arrival, how many he had on the bus, and how many hours he visited every week. I then make a big graph that depicts each Sunday of the year, divided into fifty-two and the numbers showing the ups and downs of the bus ministry. I have one man who acts as our *check-in man* and gets the information for my weekly bus sheet from each one of the bus captains as they arrive. This is then given to me and posted on a Bus Attendance Board (challenge board) at the front of the church.

As far as maintenance is concerned it could be a good idea to have your bus check-in man ask the bus captain additionally if there are any problems on his bus such as the turn signals not working, brakes going out, flat tire, etc. This could be written on a separate piece marked for maintenance or each week the bus captain

BUS CAPTAINS' REPORT   Date **MAR. 31, 1968**

NAME	START. TIME.	ARRIVAL TIME	HOURS VISITED	PASSEN-GERS
1. Appleby	8:30	9:30	4	39
2. Blong	8:45	9:50	3	75
3. Burleson	8:00	9:35	3½	31
4. Eatmon	8:30	9:40	4½	51
5. Gunnells	8:10	9:40	sick	75
6. LaVanchy	8:30	9:55	5	65
7. Maynor	8:00	9:45	2½	60
8. Mints	8:25	9:55	3	32
9. Oswalt	8:30	9:35	3	60
10. Bullington	8:30	9:48	3½	45
11. Sass	8:30	9:45	4	67
12. Schweck.	8:30	9:50	3	37
13. Williams	8:30	9:50	4	56
14. Gilmore	8:30	9:45	5	47
MISSION		9:30	1	43

Total 783

could have a mimeographed slip with various categories such as lights, brakes, knock in engine, oil pressure, overheating, a great number of blanks or check marks to indicate there was some problem. Also on this same slip you could put the information that the bus check-in man needs such as the departure time, arrival time, hours visited, etc.

The bus record is then placed in a permanent type of book that is much like a notebook and at a moment's notice you can see how many hours they have been calling, etc. We have a label maker in the church and I make each one of the bus captains a little label that has his name on it and he puts it on a plastic thing with a pin on it and wears it on Sunday morning and when he visits on Saturday. This acquaints the people with his name in print so that they can see it and call it. Dr. Hyles and several others have numbered the buses because they have so many and have a little rubber stamp with that number on it that they stamp each child's hand with as they get off. Then anyone who sees the child and feels that he looks like he is lost can simply look at his hand and guide him to the proper bus.

I have one bus captain who has an unusual name. His name is Larry Schweckendieck! Since his name is so difficult to pronounce and to spell, I put on his bus captain's sign, "Brother Larry." All the people on his route call him "Brother Larry." It is a wonderful feeling for a bus captain to walk through the neighborhood where his route is and have the children from all ends of the street call out, "Hi, Brother Larry!" "There's Brother Larry!" It is wonderful when, after a few months of working one area, you see all the fruits of your labor with many souls being saved and the children that you personally led to Christ or have had saved off your bus route coming to greet you and hug you every time you get out on the bus route.

Bus Captains' Records

I mentioned earlier in the book just a reference to the archboard that we use for the roll on the bus route. I have experimented for several years with different methods in keeping up with the people on the routes. Because you need to know who was present last week and who was present the week before, because you could get sick and someone else would have to run your route, because you might be out of town and someone else would have to visit for you, you need to have a perfectly accurate roll of your bus route including names, addresses, phone numbers, and the exact way that route is run each Sunday. In order to do this we found that the simplest way was to have an archboard which has two arched rings on it fastened at the bottom of the ring. These rings either open by a clasp or by turning them. This allows you to slip on a three-by-five card or other piece of literature that you would like to put on it. In the past I have used three-by-five cards with the holes punched in them and find there is not enough room on them to completely do what needs to be done.

The cards that are placed on these boards have the name, address, and other information as illustrated on page 72 of this book and the illustrations of various forms. One card is filled out on each child so that you can show the personal interest in the child who misses out of a family of four or five. These cards are arranged in the exact order that you drive your bus on the bus route. In other words, the first card is the first pickup, the second card is the second pickup, etc. The last card would be the last one you would pick up before you head for the church. If one of these people moves away or attends another church or dies you can simply withdraw the card by taking it off the archboard without disturbing all the other cards or messing up your records. When you add people to your route you

NEAT

NAME **George Hunnicutt**
ADDRESS 2820 Myra St.
PHONE 389-1696 AGE 7 DATE STARTED _____
DATE SAVED _____ MEMBER OF TRINITY Yes ☑ No ☐
BUS CAPTAIN DMG DATE BAPTIZED _____

ATTENDANCE:
Jan.	Feb.	March	April	May
7 14 21 28	4 11 18 25	3 10 17 24 31	7 14 21 28	5 12 19 26
.	✓ ✓ O	✓ O ✓ ✓ ✓		

3-2-68   BUS SALVATION PROSPECT

NAME Mrs. Effler
ADDRESS 21 W. 3rd St. (On Right side)
BUS CAPTAIN LKS (Initials) DATE CHILDREN STARTED TO RIDE 2-17-68
GENERAL INFORMATION Children
Robert (8); Donald (7); Patricia (5); Tommy (4)
VISITOR'S NAME _____
RESULTS _____

can simply slip them in exactly at the place they live along the route.

This way if you are ill on Saturday (when you normally visit) you can simply give the archboard to someone else and they can follow the addresses right along and visit the people for you encouraging them to come Sunday. The same is true of the Sunday run in that the bus driver who has never driven the route before can simply follow the addresses and the way they are put on the archboard.

The sample *Church Bus Ministry-Form* that appears on page 75 is one almost identical to the one that Arnold Pent developed out in Texas. I have changed it only slightly since receiving this fine idea from him for the records. At present I have this form printed up in triplicate (there are three actual pages to the form.) The first two pages are made out of paper with a carbon paper between. The final page is a cardstock and that is the one that is photographed in the book. It says, "Welcome to Sunday school, present this slip to your records." On the slip is the bus number, the bus captain's name or initials which have been previously filled in, the age of the child, name, address, parent's name, school grade (if you want it), the school name, salvation date, phone number, and one year's attendance.

The attendance is by circling the Sunday, for instance, the first Sunday, second Sunday, third Sunday, etc. The salvation date is for the pleasure of the bus captain as he looks back at the end of each year and judges what God has allowed him to do through this tremendous ministry. For instance, everyone who was saved in 1969 would have a salvation date ending with 1969. He can simply count those on his archboard and be able to see on the first day of 1970 how many people he was privileged to lead to the Lord through his faithfulness in visitation on the bus ministry. The bus triplicate forms are undated so you can start any time in the year and go for a complete year with them. You will then not have to change all of the forms at once but simply the ones that you have just started on your route exactly one year from the time you started them.

Let me explain why you have three forms and why I may add a fourth form to them. As the new child gets on the bus on Sunday morning your secretary, who is checking roll and taking attendance, looks at the house number and asks the child if he lives there, if this is his address, etc. She fills out the complete bus form which is going through to make three copies. She takes the top copy, which is yellow and says, "Welcome to Sunday school, present this slip to Sunday school teacher," and either gives this to the child, pins it on him with a straight pin, or puts in his pocket in an obvious place. As soon as the bus captain takes this child to the Sunday school class the Sunday school teacher asks for the yellow slip, sees it on the child's clothing, or in the pocket and has a complete record without her having to pump the child for information or copy it off a welcome badge that the child might be wearing. (I'm working on something now where I can add a fourth copy to this and perforate it around the name, address, only. It can then be torn off, licked, and put on the child's clothes for identification throughout the church during that first day he comes.)

The second slip in the form is blue and says, "Welcome to Sunday school, present this slip to the bus check-in man." As the bus captain arrives he gives all of his blue slips, which are new people that day, to the bus check-in man who receives the records. This man then takes this to the church office or to the person in charge and this starts and maintains a huge list of visitors and regular attenders who can be placed on a mailing list. In other words, the blue slips are a "bus people" mailing list. If you wish to mail something just

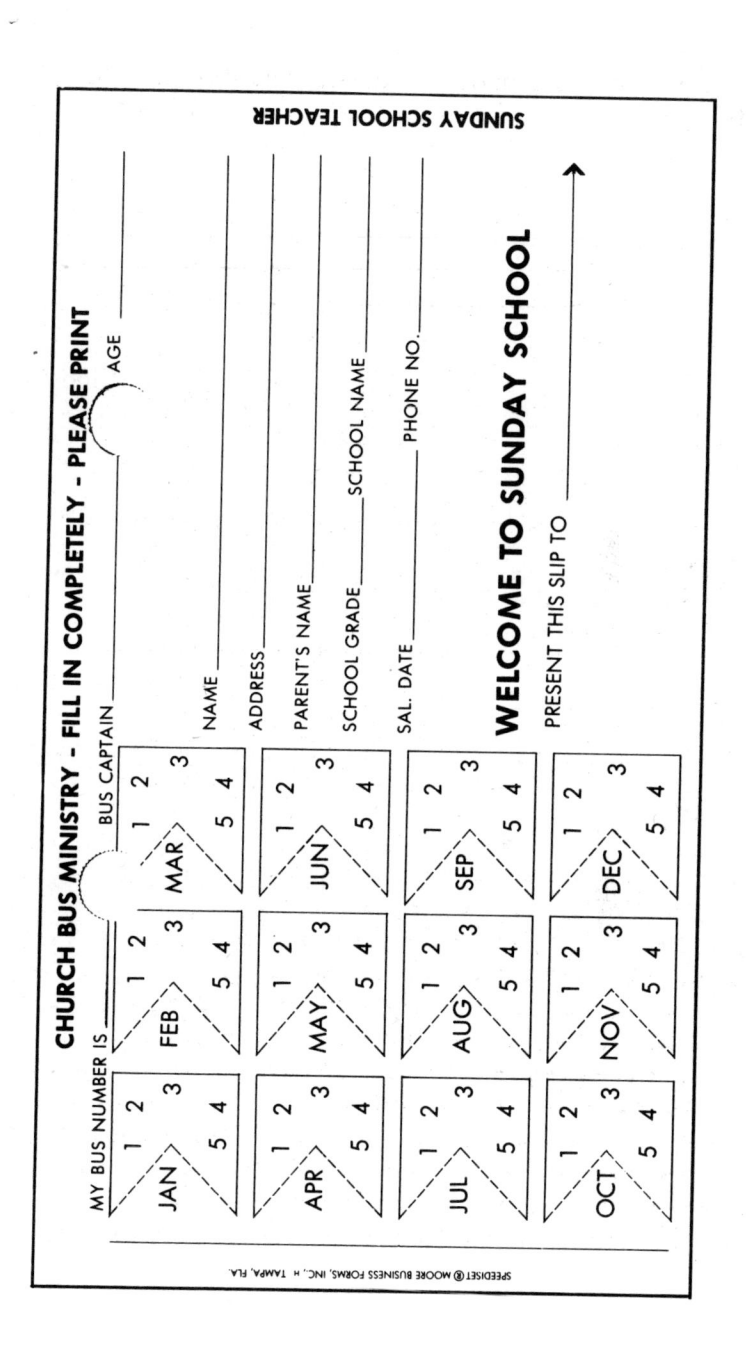

CHURCH BUS MINISTRY - FILL IN COMPLETELY - PLEASE PRINT

MY BUS NUMBER IS _____ BUS CAPTAIN _____ AGE _____

NAME _____
ADDRESS _____
PARENT'S NAME _____
SCHOOL GRADE _____ SCHOOL NAME _____
SAL. DATE _____ PHONE NO. _____

WELCOME TO SUNDAY SCHOOL

PRESENT THIS SLIP TO _____ →

SUNDAY SCHOOL TEACHER

JAN 1 2 3 4 5	FEB 1 2 3 4 5	MAR 1 2 3 4 5
APR 1 2 3 4 5	MAY 1 2 3 4 5	JUN 1 2 3 4 5
JUL 1 2 3 4 5	AUG 1 2 3 4 5	SEP 1 2 3 4 5
OCT 1 2 3 4 5	NOV 1 2 3 4 5	DEC 1 2 3 4 5

SPEEDISET® MOORE BUSINESS FORMS, INC. H TAMPA, FLA.

to the "bus people" for a contest or a special announcement then you go and find these blue slips which can be grouped according to zip codes, sections of town, alphabetical, or whatever.

There is one other form that you could print up in your church and use with the buses that I have used. That is a bus *salvation prospect form*. This form will contain the name, address, bus captain's initials, the date the children started to ride, general information, visitor's name, results. When the bus captain finds a family on their Saturday visitation that is a good prospect for salvation they can write the names down after they go through their route and put them on these prospect cards. Then on visitation night these prospects could be passed out to some of the key soul winners in your church and they could visit them that night with salvation and soul winning in view.

LAST WORDS

Since this bus ministry could change your church so much that you would not even recognize it within a few months it is wise to tell you some of the things that you might run into with this bus ministry.

The Sunday school teachers' attitude might need some help. I have had some Sunday school teachers who were extremely unhappy about their number being raised in the Sunday school class by the added children coming in on the buses. These children received very unfriendly welcomes from some of these teachers. Whenever you anticipate a bus ministry you should meet with all of your teachers and explain the scriptural motivation involved, what you plan to do, and that you expect them to cooperate and to help every way possible. For example, I had one Sunday school teacher when I came into her class with two or three five-year-olds in tow, respond to these new ones in her class thusly, "What is your birthday?" The child said nothing because she did not know her birthday. "You can't bring her in here if she doesn't know her birthday!" A couple of receptions like that in the Sunday school and the child would not want to be brought there under any circumstances. Make sure that your Sunday school teachers are ready and expecting to be crowded out to the walls with new people all the time.

Your Sunday school teachers also will become lazy as far as following up on visitation of their new prospects is concerned. (They will have many of them each Sunday if the bus ministry is worked right and therefore, they should be prepared ahead of time to keep up with the new prospects all the time.) Also, they will become lazy about visiting absentees because they feel the bus captains will be visiting them anyway. Care should be taken to express to them that the more exposure of the friendliness of the church, the personal interest of the people in the church, and the Gospel being brought by every Christian worker into that home, the better it will be for the family that lives there.

Because of the added children in your services you will find there will be more noise, more strange things (as the little boy who rode the bus and sailed paper airplanes out of the balcony during the message), more rowdiness, and *more souls saved in the services.* If you go into a bus ministry, your new buildings, whether educational or for the purpose of an auditorium, should be planned around silencing some of the noise from hymnbooks, scuffing on the floor, and the other by-products of the bus ministry.

We have found in some of the Sunday school departments it is wise to have a separate Sunday school secretary sit outside in the hall of your educational building to register the children who come in off the buses and place them into proper classes. We also find that because you're reaching out many miles in each direction from the church it is sometimes wise if you put the children who live in a certain section of town or that come off of just certain buses into the same class or department. This allows the Sunday school teacher to only have to go to one section of town for their visitation. For instance, in Trinity there were lists on the Sunday school department doors stating which bus route children should be placed in that class. This will help the Sunday school teachers immensely. If you will have the bus captains make sure and fill out completely the yellow slips on these archboard forms and give them to the children it will certainly help. (In order to get a price on these church bus ministry forms so churches can afford them I have found that I have to buy them in huge quantities of above 20,000. Approximately 500 of these forms will do four bus routes for the period of one year. If you would be interested in securing these forms I would be happy to sell them to you as I keep them in stock at my office, Route 1, Box 43, Ruskin, Florida 33570, and you can write me for prices.)

Because of all the added people and especially the children that will be brought in through the bus ministry we have had to have some of our deacons and other volunteers patrolling the buildings and buses during the services. This is especially true at night because you bring in many folks who have never been in church before or who are coming not necessarily for the reason of worshiping the Lord. In the services I have asked my bus captains to sit about every twenty feet in the midst of large concentrations of children. When you find that they have no parents there to restrain them many of the children will act up unless some adult takes the initiative to sit down with them.

If you run many buses you will find out that one of these days you will come up to the home after church is over and there will be no child on the bus to get off. A frantic bus captain will call back to the church or the pastor saying they have lost one of the children. In reality no child has ever been lost from a bus route because the child has to be somewhere. Let me give you a few tips on where to look for the child if the child is not on the bus where they are supposed to be. The child could have gone home with a relative, such as a cousin, grandmother (also a little friend). The parents could have taken the child home after Sunday school. The child may have started to walk home and would be found along the route. The child could still be in the nursery. The child could have gotten on another bus and the bus captain will find them at the end of their route and return them back to the church. Someone should be left at the church until the child is found in order to take any calls or information about it. We have had a number of these situations happen but everyone has always turned out well and no harm has ever been done.

EXAMPLES OF PEOPLE SAVED

Roderick Sumner was a little boy twelve years of age who came two Sundays and was saved the second Sunday on the bus route. His mother had also received Christ as personal Saviour at the church. Suddenly he became ill and when taken to the hospital he was found to have a tumor at the base of his skull. He went blind and was operated on for the tumor but doctors found it an impossible situation. Roderick witnessed to all of the nurses and the doctors in the hospital and most of all to his unsaved dad. In approximately five weeks after he was saved, he went to be with the Lord Jesus. It was just a few months until his father also received Christ as his Saviour. Ironically enough, within two years Roderick's father also passed away with cancer. He went to be with the boy he loved so much, and to Heaven with the Lord who gave him so much. All of this happened because one faithful bus captain knocked on a door and invited the child to come.

One of the Sloan children had been saved on the bus route and I did the follow-up by knocking on the door to find out about baptismal permission. I found out quickly that the mother had not been saved and led her to Christ at the kitchen table. She came forward the following Sunday and made profession of faith and was baptized. The next Sunday her husband who was a Marine sergeant in Jacksonville came to church. This big tough sergeant sat through four services of the church and then came bawling down the aisle and received Christ personally as his Saviour. It was only a couple of weeks before this man volunteered to teach a Sunday school class and had cleaned up his life and was living for Christ and completely sold out for Jesus. He then took his own bus route and started a Sunday school class and a Good News Club in his home. (He was transferred to Vietnam and in Vietnam tried to lead his entire squad to the Lord. He has since returned to the state of North Carolina and is actively serving the Lord.)

Mrs. Bernard's little girl had been saved at church. The bus captain was there making his visit when I knocked at the door. Mr. Bernard was in the Navy and was a great big tall Lutheran man. When I dealt with him in front of his wife and the children he responded by asking Christ to come into his heart and his wife rededicated her life as a backslidden Christian. He followed the Lord in baptism and for a cold, dead Lutheran made a mighty good Baptist! I recall that he used to sit at the very back of the church but within three or four months, he was sitting on the second row of the church saying "Amen" and raising his hand at the points of the sermon that he enjoyed. These folks that I have previously mentioned, after being saved, no longer rode the buses but instead drove their own cars to the church.

The first Sunday that the Warrens came to church, he accepted Christ as his personal Saviour. Brother Gray had the joy of leading his wife to the Lord in the home and they have become active members of the church as well as all of their children having been saved in the church. Now both Mr. and Mrs. Warren teach Sunday school on our Bible school faculty.

Mr. and Mrs. Ayers were first contacted by one of our bus captains who led him to Christ in the home. After making profession of faith and being baptized, in a few months his wife came to Christ and the family is now in the church.

Mr. Klemm was a Lutheran from the Chicago area. He had his religion and was not interested in anything else. This is what he told Dr. Gray as he returned the call that the children had made to Sunday school via our buses. One of the children had been saved on the buses and therefore Dr. Gray was seeking permission for baptism. At the kitchen table, he had the joy of leading this lost Lutheran to Christ. His wife rededicated her life to the Lord and now this man has a very responsible position in the city and is a superintendent of one of the departments where he and his wife teach Sunday school. He is also a deacon.

Does it pay to win people on bus routes? I would have to say joyously and thankfully, it certainly does!

Let me give you an example of one bus route being started. We had prayed for sometime about starting a bus route out in Jacksonville Beach. This is a long way from the church and would require at least forty-five to fifty minutes of driving each way for the bus even after they picked up all of their bus riders. One of our men moved to the beach area and was within five miles of the beach. He consented to start the route. For two weeks (which is my usual policy), I visited with him and showed him how to make the visitation calls and to start winning souls there on the route. The first

Sunday there was just a handful, something over ten, on the bus. The next Sunday it went up to nineteen or twenty.

The second week that we were visiting on the route, I noticed two children walking down a dirt road. I stopped beside them and asked them if they went to Sunday school. They said, "No." I asked them to point to their house. They did and met us around the corner as we started to talk to the mother. The mother consented for them to come to Sunday school on the bus. Within a week or two, all of the children had come and several had been saved on the route. The mother had been led to Christ by the wife of the bus captain and within three weeks the father had trusted Christ also under the testimony of the bus captain on the route. On the fifth Sunday of his route, this bus captain had sixty-one on the route and seven were saved that Sunday from his route.

Chapter 5

Individual Questions and Comments

1. What about opposition to the bus ministry from the people in the church?
ANSWER: There will be many folks in the church who will not think it is worth it to dirty their church with the little ragamuffins that would come in on the buses. I am sure the Lord Jesus would not feel this way but yet there are some so-called Christians who would. I personally feel that the emphasis should be on the soul winning and the bus ministry will naturally fall in line.

2. Will the bus ministry pay its way?
ANSWER: No, it will not. I recall in my first church that one of the dear deacons, whom I'm sure was well meaning, had mentioned to me in a rather confidential tone that he had never known anybody to stay in the church who had come in on a bus. This is, I am sure, because they did not take a real interest in the route or else it is because they did not do it long enough.
Because of the local problem of people moving, in some cases it has taken a year or two to really reach the entire family with the Gospel on the bus route (in Jacksonville). The children are usually won and attracted into the church through the bus ministry. In our present pastorate (in Ruskin, Florida) we have seen people drawn into the church through the bus

ministry, whole families coming to Christ, most of these then driving their cars and becoming active Christians in the period of just a few months rather than years.

3. How many does a bus route run before you split it?

ANSWER: Around fifty or sixty for three Sundays or so. Or if the route is too long, getting in late, getting home late, it may be only running thirty on the route, but it should be split. The length of the route is then holding it back and rather than lose half of the people and build one route it would be wise to split it and get another bus captain for the other part of the route.

4. What time do the buses start picking up and how long does it take them to get home?

ANSWER: Our buses start picking up at 8:30 a.m. This is approximately one hour before Sunday school. It makes them get in starting at 9:30 until 9:50. Our Sunday school starts at 9:45. To have them all in by 9:45 is our ideal. It takes a little less time to get them home because of not waiting for people to get back on the bus.

5. How many buses do you own?

ANSWER: We only own four of our seventeen buses. We rent thirteen of them. Dr. Faulkner at Highland Park Baptist Church in Chattanooga rents ALL of his buses. Dr. Hyles in Hammond, Indiana, owns most of his buses. If you get enough buses, it will pay you to hire a good Christian man to maintain the fleet of buses. (Some folks have found that they can use a man part time as a janitor and maintenance man as well as a person to work on the buses.)

6. Do you have a regular bus captains' meeting?

ANSWER: No, we do not. *MANY SHOULD*, however, especially during the early days of your bus ministry. We meet with the bus captains as often as needed. Sometimes we need to meet weekly with them because of a contest or a particular situation. At that time, I either meet with them after the service at night or else I meet with them during the Teachers' Meeting on Wednesday night from 7:00 to 7:30. Anyone who is absent receives a copy of the things discussed in the meeting. I usually send a copy to everyone so that they will have notes on what was said. I also send a copy to the pastor and to myself.

7. Do you use any <u>direct mail in your promotion of</u> the bus ministry?

ANSWER: <u>Yes!</u> Whenever a child comes the first time he is put on a promotional mailing list. We have found that we can boost our Sunday school attendance fifty to seventy-five by simply sending out one postcard announcing some special day or somebody that is going to be there.

8. What if someone wants to use your bus and someone else has planned to use it for another party?

ANSWER: I have a schedule for the buses that we own indicating the groups wanting to use it for parties on various dates. They must check with this schedule and with me before they are allowed to use it for field trips or any other use. I never allow groups outside the church to use our buses.

9. How do you keep your buses properly?

ANSWER: We leave them at a gas station where they are to be swept, gassed up and ready to go every week. (We also keep them properly insured at all times to protect our interest in case someone is hurt on the buses. We have had probably two small accidents in the last four years on the buses. One involved a tooth being knocked out and another a cut on the forehead.) Some feel it best to leave all your buses at your church for the advertising effect. Get some lock caps if you do.

Some also leave them at the driver's or captain's home.

10. How many people do you feel you can get for each hour of calling on Saturday?

ANSWER: I added up the hours of calling and found it amounts to usually ten people per hour will come on Sunday for each hour called by our bus captains.

11. How can you tell whose bus goes in what area?

ANSWER: We have a bus information sheet that is mimeographed and given to several people—to each one of the bus captains, to the church secretaries, put in a prominent place in the visitation room, to the pastor, also a copy for the pastor's home and my home. This bus information sheet contains the following information: (1) The bus captain—his address and telephone number. (2) The bus type, such as 1965 Chevrolet, Ward Body, 66-passengers. (3) The owner—Mr. So-and-So, his address, and phone number. (4) The driver—Mr. So-and-So, address and phone number. (5) The cost of the bus. Example—$20.00 per Sunday.

12. Do you know of other helpful material that is available on the bus ministry?

ANSWER: Yes. There is a lecture on the bus ministry by Brother Jim Lyons of the First Baptist Church of Hammond, Indiana, at the 1965 Pastors' Conference that is taken down on tape. Also there is one by Brother Charles Hand of the First Baptist Church of Hammond in a Pastors' Conference since then. Also I have one taken down at the Southwide Baptist Fellowship in 1967 and in 1969 that I delivered on the Bus Ministry. These may be secured from the Tape Ministry Supply, Loren Cody Dawson, Box 157, Bath, Illinois 62617. The approximate cost of one reel of tape is all you pay for this, which is about $3.00. On the return side of the tape, you may get one of the many sermons that he has recorded in Bible conferences and other ministries. Dr. Jack Hyles has a 10-page chapter on the bus ministry in his book, *The Hyles Church Manual,* published by the Sword of the Lord Publishers. Also, he has several books, *Let's Build an Evangelistic Church, How to Boost Your Sunday School Attendance,* and other interesting books that would be helpful along this same line but do *not* directly refer to a bus ministry in detail. Dr. Hyles is also coming out with quite a large clothbound book on the bus ministry which, at this writing, has yet to be released. It will be well worth your purchasing, I'm sure.

13. How do you feel about splitting bus routes?

ANSWER: I feel like the old expression, "We multiply when we divide." If you will divide a route and get a good man on both routes, you will have twice as many on the route.

14. What about some bus promotion ideas?

ANSWER: If you are buying your own fleet of buses and have the means to do so, I would suggest that you pick a color for your buses that is not used by everyone else. If possible, a *peculiar* color that is very pleasing would be nice, and, of course, painting the name of the church and the name of the pastor on the bus as well as the address. I also have used on the buses we rent a system whereby we have taken black canvas and painted with white letters the name Trinity Baptist Church and put them on with snaps on the side of the bus. This involves a bus contractor allowing you to put snaps into the side of the bus with a little drill. Most of them will do this. Also we have printed up some signs, with the names of the bus captains such as "Williams," and put this in the front of the bus so the children will be looking for the name of the bus captain. Since they have seen his name on the name tag, they will know how to spell it and they will be looking for Brother Williams' bus.

Here is another tip. Although I have not tried this I feel it will work. I know of two men who have been trying it and it seems to work very well for them. That is, to establish some Good News Clubs, a little Bible club with a flannelgraph lesson, in someone's house out on the bus route. At the close of the club each week the person in charge is to ask how many children do not attend Sunday school and to invite them to come back and meet at the house that coming Sunday at such and such a time and a bus will pick them up. Sometimes there is an added incentive by giving a colored piece of paper or a ticket or some other thing to the child and saying that they will receive a free gift if they will give this to the bus captain on Sunday morning. The free gift can be a book marker or anything along that line.

SUMMARY

In one sitting you can learn the majority of the things needed to start a bus ministry. However, I have found it imperative to constantly review several ideas and details. Keep constantly the basic philosophy of a bus ministry in mind as you visit and plan your routes. (1) The motivation—the scriptural injunction of Matthew 22:9. (2) The Quantity Trio—quantity calls equals quantity people equals quantity souls. (3) Go to it!

IS JESUS GOD?

BY DR. JOHN R. RICE
205 PAGES, PRICE $3.50

The first chapter, "Is Jesus God?" was written in answer to a modernist who heard Dr. Rice preach in a tent revival campaign in Brooklyn, N. Y. A burning, convicting chapter showing how no one has a right to be called a Christian or even claim to be a friend of Christ except as he accepts Christ as the virgin-born Saviour and the Bible as the very Word of God.

Chapter two, "A Letter to a Modernist," is a second letter to the modernist, dealing with the complaints of the modernists about idolizing the Bible, about narrowness, about being slaves to the letter of the Bible, and showing how Jesus and His disciples regarded and rebuked infidels and unbelievers.

Chapter three is "The Virgin-Born Saviour." Here is explicit proof that the Bible categorically and repeatedly affirms the virgin birth of Christ; that His virgin birth is implied throughout the Scriptures. Here the five principal arguments of unbelievers against the virgin birth are answered conclusively, convincingly, thrillingly.

Chapter four is "Old Testament Prophecies Miraculously Fulfilled in Christ." From these clearly stated prophecies we have infallible proof of the deity of Christ and the inspiration of the Bible. There is wonderful strengthening for the Christian's faith and powerful ammunition against unbelievers.

Chapter five is "The Resurrection of Jesus Christ." Possibly the strongest in the book, this will convince every open-minded reader, we believe, that the resurrection is the most easily provable fact about Jesus Christ. There are literally, as the Bible says, "many infallible proofs;" here they are given.

The last long, tremendous chapter is "What Is Wrong With a Modernist." Shows he is an infidel, not a believer; a lost sinner, not a Christian; a fool, not a wise man; an insincere hypocrite, not an honest doubter; and is under an awful curse of God.

Honest scoffers and doubters can be converted. Word has already come from preachers led back to faith in Christ and the Bible, away from the modernism taught them in seminaries, through these articles when published in THE SWORD OF THE LORD. We believe this book will save thousands from ship-wreck of the faith. Ought to be in the hands of every ministerial student, every modernist preacher and, in fact, every earnest Christian worker.

Beautifully printed and bound; large, clear type; simple, pungent Christian language. Irrefutable proof, a mighty challenge! Help spread this book. Price **$3.50**

ALWAYS REJOICING

By John R. Rice

Nine chapters on the way of constant happiness and peace for a Christian.

CHAPTER TITLES:

1. Always Rejoicing;
2. The Heavenly Language of Flowers (written when Dr. Rice lay abed five weeks with a fractured skull);
3. Count Your Blessings!
4. My Jesus, Your Jesus;
5. The Angel Said, "Merry Christmas, Everybody!"
6. Whosoever and Whatsoever When You Pray;
7. "A Woman of Canaan" or How to Get What You Need;
8. Brotherly Love Covers the Multitude of Sins;
9. "There Remaineth Therefore a Rest to the People of God."

$3.00

Robert Sumner said: *"It seems incredible to suppose that any child of God would be disappointed upon obtaining and digesting* ALWAYS REJOICING."

Introduction by Dr. Lee Roberson

For many people it will make the difference between success and failure, between happiness and despair. A beautiful gift volume, a comfort for the distressed, help for those in trouble, inspiration for the discouraged, heart warming and tears and laughter for Christians.

Order from your bookseller or from

SWORD OF THE LORD PUBLISHERS
Box 1099, Murfreesboro, Tenn. 37130

HAVE YOU READ THESE BOOKS?

BIBLE GIANTS TESTED...

by Dr. John R. Rice

"Great Characters of Scripture as Each Was Tried and Revealed by Some Great Crisis," stirring biographical sketches of men of the Bible, dealing with the lives of Jacob, Caleb, King Saul, Jehoshaphat, Elijah, John the Baptist, Peter and Paul. Dr. Bob Ketcham, leader in the General Association of Regular Baptist Churches, says:

"*The entire book is extremely valuable, but in my judgment, Chapter 4 on Jehoshaphat is worth the price of the book many times over . . . you have presented it in an extraordinarily able fashion.*"

A book that is bound to build character and strengthen convictions. Buy several copies as gifts NOW!

$3.50

The Golden Path to Successful Personal Soul Winning

By Dr. John R. Rice

Other books have been written beforehand on soul winning, but none have considered the subject so completely as does this beautiful large volume from the burning heart and prolific pen of the "dean of American evangelists." While touching on collective soul-winning efforts through the church and united campaign, this book deals principally with *personal* soul winning, treating exhaustively the how, when, where, why and who of it all. Every Christian should read and own a copy of this, another great manual. *Moody Monthly* says, "The author has a compelling passion for souls." 314 pages, scenic cover, hard binding.

$3.50

Sword of the Lord Publishers
Murfreesboro, Tennessee 37130

THE SCARLET SIN

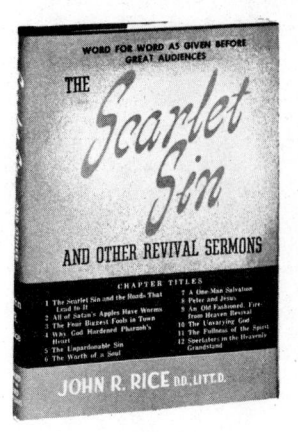

This book, **The Scarlet Sin and Other Revival Sermons** was immediately and magnificently popular when it appeared in 1946. There are several reasons:

First, these sermons are stenographically reported, word for word, just as given before great revival audiences in various places in America. You feel the warmth of the Spirit's presence, the pulse of the great listening crowd, the convicting power of the Holy Spirit as you read these sermons. They were not dictated in the study, but taken down word for word in the midst of God's blessing and are printed for the first time in book form. When printed in **The Sword of the Lord** they brought many, many letters of commendation.

Second, the titles of the sermons themselves make you want to read the book.

CHAPTER TITLES

1. The Scarlet Sin and the Roads That Lead to It
2. All of Satan's Apples Have Worms
3. The Four Biggest Fools in Town
4. Why God Hardened Pharoah's Heart
5. The Unpardonable Sin
6. The Worth of a Soul
7. One-Man Salvation
8. Peter and Jesus
9. A Fire-from-Heaven Revival
10. The Unvarying God
11. The Fullness of the Holy Spirit
12. Spectators in the Heavenly Grandstand

Young people will read this book. They heard these sermons as preached in great revivals and Youth for Christ meetings. Hundreds were saved as they heard them. Lost men will be intrigued by these chapter titles. It is an ideal book to put into the hands of young people, hardened sinners, and backslidden Christians who need help. There are messages both for sinners and saints, sermons to bring conviction and salvation on the one hand, or to deepen the prayer life and soul-winning passion of those already saved, on the other hand. This is a big book, 254 pages, with twelve full-length sermons taken down word for word as preached before great audiences, with an attractive cloth cover in scarlet.

Price only **$3.50**

Our Beautiful "Catering" Book:

Favorite Chapters of the Bible

By DR. JOHN R. RICE

Yes, at our request, folks made known those portions of Scripture they liked best, those which they wished for Dr. Rice to discuss, and so he cheerfully "catered" to their expressed desires, and came up with this most attractive, large volume. Here are "50 Heart-Warming Messages on 23 of the Best-Loved Chapters in the Bible," so that surely any potential reader will find at least one particular chapter "catering" to his personal desire or preference, while, at the same time, getting a rich blessing from reading the entire volume. If one approaches this volume not yet having any preference among portions of Scripture, the reading of these illuminating chapters will help in the selection of one as proving most dear to the heart.

The 50 chapters are grouped under twelve major sections, as follows:

I. Creation, the Fall, Murder, the Flood—Gen. 1-6
II. The Ten Commandments—Exod. 20
III. Favorite Psalms—Nos. 1,23,37,91
IV. Christmas Scripture—Matt. 2, Luke 2
V. The Sermon on the Mount—Matt. 5-7
VI. Christ Seeking the Lost—Luke 15
VII. John 3
VIII. John 14
IX. The Olivet Discourse—Matt. 24
X. The Trial and Crucifixion of Christ—Matt. 27
XI. No Condemnation...No Separation...for God's Children—Rom. 8
XII. The Resurrection Chapter—I Cor. 15

Each major section is prefaced with appropriate full-page drawings, with a listing of chapter titles—a most attractive, large and compact volume! 462 pages.

4 75

"Dr. Rice Has Done It Again!" in...

GREAT TRUTHS
FOR SOUL WINNERS
By Dr. John R. Rice

Consider These Chapter Titles

1. Winning Your Loved Ones
2. God's Fruit Trees, Soul Winners
3. Excuses for Disobedience About Soul Winning
4. Getting Sinners to Heaven Who Ought to Be in Hell
5. Raising the Dead
6. The Kind of Preaching We Need
7. God Hath Chosen the Weak for Soul Winners
8. Soul Winner, Take Sides With God
9. Ashamed of Jesus?
10. Soul Winner, "Open Thy Mouth Wide"
11. A Fire in the Bones

301 Pages **$3.50**

SWORD OF THE LORD
Box 1099
Murfreesboro, Tennessee 37130

Read what Dr. Robert L. Sumner, well-known, nationwide evangelist, says about this volume:

"Dr. Rice has done it again! There is a freshness, a warmth, a passion on these pages that is difficult for a reviewer to describe in print. These messages get under the skin in a manner that will probably make the most successful soul winner feel that he really hasn't gotten started in this all-important business. They will encourage the timid, challenge the self-satisfied, instruct the novice, bless the discouraged, offer hope to the defeated and thrill every child of God who longs to do the will of God."

"Yes," as Dr. Sumner concludes his good review, "DR. RICE HAS DONE IT AGAIN!"

COMMENTARIES
verse-by-verse
Dr. John R. Rice

$5.95 EACH

THE KING OF THE JEWS, Commentary on Matthew. Of it, Dr. R. G. Lee says: *"Of all the commentaries on Matthew's gospel that I have read and studied during the years I have been a pastor, I must say this is, for me, the best."* Dr. Bob Jones, Sr., called it *". . .the most readable commentary I have ever seen."* 504 pages.

FILLED WITH THE SPIRIT, Commentary on Acts. Concerning this volume, Dr. Tom Malone says, *"By far your best work thus far. . . ."* Dr. Lee Roberson writes, *". . .practical and refreshing! . . ."* Dr. Jack Hyles comments: *"Makes you feel that you actually can live in the 20th century as the Christians did in the first century. . . ."* 555 pages.

THE SON OF MAN, Commentary on Luke. A portion of Dr. Robert Wells' review says, *"The commentary on any given passage is short, concise, to the point, and unfailingly helpful. There are interesting illustrations and there is some application. Other scholars are quoted . . . but basically the work is indicative of Dr. Rice's independent thinking."* 563 pages.

THE CHURCH OF GOD AT CORINTH, Commentary on I and II Corinthians. This attractively bound and jacketed volume is arranged for either convenient consecutive reading or intensive or topical study, reproducing the entire Scripture text by chapters and sections, interspersed invariably with enlightening comments, expositions, and appropriate applications. 271 pages.

SWORD OF THE LORD FOUNDATION
BOX 1099, MURFREESBORO, TENNESSEE 37130

BLOOD and TEARS on the Stairway

Messages on the Way to God, Forgiveness and Heaven

By Evangelist John R. Rice. In his brief Introduction the author gives the motivation and purpose for this volume:
"I was moved to tears as I saw the heart hunger, and most often the false hope, I fear, of those pitiful people climbing the 'Holy Stairs' at Rome kissing each step before climbing it on bruised knees. Oh, how many saw through the devices, the trappings, and found a Saviour who saves by simple faith all who come to Him in the heart?

187 PAGES

3⁵⁰

NOTE THE STRIKING CHAPTER TITLES!

1. Blood and Tears on the Stairway
2. Snakes in the Camp!
3. The Jericho Crook Saved Up a Tree
4. "Christ Died for Our Sins"
5. Already Condemned!
6. "I've Wandered Far Away From Home"
7. "Seek Ye the Lord"
8. Heaven Is Waiting
9. Calling You, Sinner
10. "Choose You This Day"

"I will never be done telling to sinners the truths taught here! Christ is the way to Heaven! He died for sinners! All who penitently seek Him, find Him as precious Saviour. If you choose Him, trust Him, take Him, He is yours!

"Yesterday I saw a score or more sinners come to Christ with such preaching as is here! Will you see that unsaved sinners are invited to read, are enlisted to read these messages?

"Here is seed spread abroad! It is sown with tears. May much of it fall in the good ground of hungry hearts and bring forth fruit to salvation in many."

Let's face it! Some sinners are too proud to even receive a gospel tract, let alone read one! But if you present them with a handsomely bound book of sermons like this, their ego is inflated, and they very often will take the time to read it, and are thereby brought to conviction and salvation, together with the help of our prayers.

And, too, this is good model preaching to sinners for ministerial students and busy pastors. An excellent gift volume! 187 pages.

Order from your bookseller or from

Sword of the Lord Box 1099, Murfreesboro, Tenn. 37130